W9-CIA-459

Is Offshore Oil Drilling Worth the Risks?

Hal Marcovitz

INCONTROVERSY

ReferencePoint
Press®

San Diego, CA

About the Author
A former newspaper reporter and columnist, Hal Marcovitz is the author of more than 150 books for young readers. He makes his home in Chalfont, Pennsylvania, with his wife Gail and daughter Ashley.

For more information, contact:
ReferencePoint Press, Inc.
PO Box 27779
San Diego, CA 92198
www.ReferencePointPress.com

Picture Credits
AP Images: 16, 27, 47, 74
© Corbis/Bettmann: 22
© Corbis/Bevil Knapp: 63
© Corbis/Ted Soqui: 32
Julie Dermansky/Science Photo Library: 58, 77
Maury Aaseng: 13, 43, 72
USCG/Science Photo Library: 7

LIBRARY OF CONGRESS CATALOGING-IN-PUBLICATION DATA

Marcovitz, Hal.
  Is offshore oil drilling worth the risks? / Hal Marcovitz.
    p. cm. — (In controversy)
  Includes bibliographical references and index.
  ISBN-13: 978-1-60152-143-9 (hardback)
  ISBN-10: 1-60152-143-X (hardback)
  1. Offshore oil well drilling—Juvenile literature. 2. Oil spills—Environmental aspects—Juvenile literature. I. Title.
  TN871.3.M37 2011
  363.738'2—dc22
                                                    2010037854

Contents

Foreword

I n 2008, as the U.S. economy and economies worldwide were falling into the worst recession since the Great Depression, most Americans had difficulty comprehending the complexity, magnitude, and scope of what was happening. As is often the case with a complex, controversial issue such as this historic global economic recession, looking at the problem as a whole can be overwhelming and often does not lead to understanding. One way to better comprehend such a large issue or event is to break it into smaller parts. The intricacies of global economic recession may be difficult to understand, but one can gain insight by instead beginning with an individual contributing factor such as the real estate market. When examined through a narrower lens, complex issues become clearer and easier to evaluate.

This is the idea behind ReferencePoint Press's *In Controversy* series. The series examines the complex, controversial issues of the day by breaking them into smaller pieces. Rather than looking at the stem cell research debate as a whole, a title would examine an important aspect of the debate such as *Is Stem Cell Research Necessary?* or *Is Embryonic Stem Cell Research Ethical?* By studying the central issues of the debate individually, researchers gain a more solid and focused understanding of the topic as a whole.

Each book in the series provides a clear, insightful discussion of the issues, integrating facts and a variety of contrasting opinions for a solid, balanced perspective. Personal accounts and direct quotes from academic and professional experts, advocacy groups, politicians, and others enhance the narrative. Sidebars add depth to the discussion by expanding on important ideas and events. For quick reference, a list of key facts concludes every chapter. Source notes, an annotated organizations list, bibliography, and index provide student researchers with additional tools for papers and class discussion.

The *In Controversy* series also challenges students to think critically about issues, to improve their problem-solving skills, and to sharpen their ability to form educated opinions. As President Barack Obama stated in a March 2009 speech, success in the twenty-first century will not be measurable merely by students' ability to "fill in a bubble on a test but whether they possess 21st century skills like problem-solving and critical thinking and entrepreneurship and creativity." Those who possess these skills will have a strong foundation for whatever lies ahead.

No one can know for certain what sort of world awaits today's students. What we can assume, however, is that those who are inquisitive about a wide range of issues; open-minded to divergent views; aware of bias and opinion; and able to reason, reflect, and reconsider will be best prepared for the future. As the international development organization Oxfam notes, "Today's young people will grow up to be the citizens of the future: but what that future holds for them is uncertain. We can be quite confident, however, that they will be faced with decisions about a wide range of issues on which people have differing, contradictory views. If they are to develop as global citizens all young people should have the opportunity to engage with these controversial issues."

In Controversy helps today's students better prepare for tomorrow. An understanding of the complex issues that drive our world and the ability to think critically about them are essential components of contributing, competing, and succeeding in the twenty-first century.

Crisis in the Gulf

S tephen Davis worked on the *Deepwater Horizon* just four days. He had found a job as a welder on the offshore exploration oil platform in the Gulf of Mexico. On April 20, 2010, Davis had just completed a 12-hour shift. He ate dinner, called his fiancée back home in San Antonio, Texas, and settled into bed.

Just 15 minutes later, a terrible explosion shook the rig. Davis knew instantly he was in danger. He jumped out of bed, threw on a life jacket, grabbed his shoes, and headed for the deck. Emerging topside, he saw chaos. "People were panicking," he says. "They would look at you and just jump into the water. You could understand why if you looked behind you and saw all these explosions, you would think you were either going to burn up or jump."[1]

Davis scrambled to the edge of the deck. Some 60 feet (18m) below, he saw a lifeboat. He jumped into the water and paddled to the boat where the other survivors hauled him aboard. Minutes later, the lifeboat made its way to the *Damon Bankston*, a supply ship that was anchored nearby. From the deck of the *Bankston*, Davis saw flames completely engulf the *Deepwater Horizon*. "We actually watched the derrick melt from the starboard side of the rig as they airlifted the guys out," he says. "It was horrid, it was overwhelming, it was unbelievable."[2]

The *Deepwater Horizon* employed 126 workers. Eleven died in the blast and another 17 were injured.

Eclipsing Other Spills

Seven months before the explosion, the *Deepwater Horizon* had accomplished an engineering achievement unprecedented in the history of the oil industry: Sitting atop a mile (1.6km) of water, the rig drilled deep below the bottom of the sea, withdrawing oil from a depth of 35,000 feet (10,668m)—nearly 7 miles (11km) below the seabed. BP, the British-based oil company formerly known as British Petroleum, had invested $350 million in the rig.

BP had big plans for the *Deepwater Horizon,* hoping it would help provide oil to an international consumer base that burns through some 1.7 billion gallons (6.4 billion L) of gasoline a day.

However, things had gone terribly wrong in the weeks leading up to April 20. A series of engineering errors, lack of government oversight, and other mishaps resulted in the explosion and a subsequent environmental horror story: After the explosion, it took BP 85 days to plug the well. In the meantime, an estimated 5 million barrels—or about 210 million gallons (795 million L)—of crude oil gushed into the Gulf of Mexico. The oil fouled the coastlines of several states, killing birds and other coastal wildlife as well as marine life in the gulf. "These waters should be jumping with fish and shrimp and there's just nothing there," said commercial fisherman Frank Lensmyer a month after the explosion. "I've been fishing here for 25 years and I've never seen anything like this. It's very, very sad."[3]

Firefighting boats douse the flames of the burning Deepwater Horizon *oil rig after the rig exploded and caught fire in the Gulf of Mexico in April 2010. Eleven workers died, 17 more were injured, and millions of gallons of oil poured into the gulf.*

The amount of oil that spilled into the gulf easily eclipsed similar oil spills—most significantly, the 1989 accident involving the tanker *Exxon Valdez*, in which 11 million gallons (41.6 million L) of oil were spilled into Prince William Sound in Alaska. Says Marcie Keever, an official of the environmental group Friends of the Earth,

> This tragedy is a stark reminder of the human, environmental, and economic costs of offshore oil drilling. Not only are oil spills extremely harmful to marine life, they also put coastal communities and local industries such as commercial and recreational fishing at risk. The explosion aboard the Deepwater Horizon and the oil spill should dispel any assertions that expanded offshore oil drilling is either safe or environmentally friendly.[4]

Expansion of Offshore Drilling

Despite the incredible shock of the accident and the wide-ranging environmental implications, the international oil industry has remained committed to offshore drilling. Worldwide, some 2,900 rigs are in operation, half of them located offshore of the United States. Most are either in the Gulf of Mexico or along the Alaskan coastline.

Indeed, in the months leading up to the *Deepwater Horizon* accident, President Barack Obama announced plans to open 230 miles (379km) along the Atlantic coastline to offshore drilling. For years, oil companies have been prohibited from erecting rigs in that area. Obama also proposed opening additional areas along the Alaska coastline to offshore drilling. Expanding offshore drilling, he said, would be a vital component of America's energy security—given that more than half of America's oil is imported from the Middle East and other volatile corners of the planet. "We're announcing the expansion of offshore oil and gas exploration," said the president, "but in ways that balance the need to harness domestic energy resources and the need to protect America's natural resources."[5]

"This tragedy [Deepwater Horizon] is a stark reminder of the human, environmental, and economic costs of offshore oil drilling."[4]

— Marcie Keever, an official of the environmental group Friends of the Earth.

Frightening Journey

Obama made those remarks on March 31, 2010. Twenty days later, things did not seem so secure on the deck of the *Deepwater Horizon.* Also aboard that evening was Mike Williams, the chief electronics technician. Seconds before the explosion, Williams was standing on one side of a heavy steel door. As he reached for the handle of the door, he heard a hissing sound. Suddenly, the door blew open, knocking Williams across the room. "I'm up against a wall, when I finally come around, with a door on top of me," Williams recalled. "And I remember thinking to myself, 'You know . . . this is it. I'm going to die right here.'"[6]

Williams scrambled to his feet, grabbed a life jacket, and started making his way to the deck. It was a long, frightening journey. As the rig shook with one explosion after another, Williams was often knocked off his feet. In fact, for most of the trip to the deck Williams crawled on hands and knees. Now on deck, Williams found himself one of the last rig workers still on board. With explosions going off everywhere, Williams made it to the edge and jumped.

Now bobbing in the choppy, chaotic waters, Williams was still very much in danger as flaming debris seemed to be falling everywhere. And then, miraculously, Williams heard a voice. "I remember a real faint voice of, 'Over here, over here.' I thought, 'What in the world is that?'" Williams recalls. "And the next thing I know, he grabbed my lifejacket and flipped me over into this small open bow boat. I didn't know who he was, I didn't know where he'd come from, I didn't care. I was now out of the water."[7] Williams's saviors were four men in a small fishing boat who had been sailing in the vicinity of the *Deepwater Horizon* when the rig exploded.

> "We're announcing the expansion of offshore oil and gas exploration, but in ways that balance the need to harness domestic energy resources and the need to protect America's natural resources."[5]
>
> — U.S. president Barack Obama shortly before the BP spill.

Strong Differences of Opinion

In the weeks following the *Deepwater Horizon* disaster, Obama ordered a temporary moratorium on deepwater oil exploration so that safety checks could be made. During the moratorium, the oil industry stood steadfast in its support for offshore drilling while opponents remained convinced that offshore drilling presents a significant danger to the environment of America's coastlines.

Facts

- The *Deepwater Horizon* had been employed in various oil explorations in the Gulf of Mexico for seven years. Prior to the April 20, 2010, explosion, no worker had ever been seriously injured on the mobile rig.

- The *Deepwater Horizon* stood 378 feet (115m), top to bottom; after the initial explosions, the rig burned for two days before sinking.

- Flames from the *Deepwater Horizon* shot as much as 300 feet (91m) into the sky and were visible from 35 miles (56km) away.

What Are the Origins of the Offshore Oil Controversy?

L ess than a century after oil drillers found a way to draw crude from below the seabed, offshore oil production had emerged as an important component of America's energy supply. By the late 1960s more than 1,000 offshore oil wells were in operation along the American shoreline, most of which were found in the Gulf of Mexico off the coast of Louisiana. At the time, about 100 wells were in operation along the West Coast, most off the coast of California but a few along the Oregon and Washington shorelines as well. Meanwhile, across the globe, oil companies were pursuing promising reserves off the coasts of Australia and North Africa as well as in the Persian Gulf in the Middle East. At the time, much of the attention in the oil exploration world was focused on the North Sea, a 300,000-square-mile area (777,000 square km) of the North Atlantic located between Great Britain and Norway.

Until the 1960s a major spill from an offshore well had never occurred. Industry officials had designed safety features into the offshore drilling operations and were confident that the risk of a leak, known in the jargon of the industry as a "blowout," was minimal. "It's a rare possibility," one industry insider told the *Los Angeles Times* in 1965. "Very remote."[8] Specifically, engineers were confident that a device known as a blowout preventer would cut off a leak before the well emitted large quantities of crude. The blowout preventer sits atop the wellhead on the sea floor. In the event of a leak, valves in the blowout preventer are supposed to close, shutting off the flow of oil to the surface.

Despite such failsafe measures, in 1969—less than four years later—the fallibility of offshore oil drilling was exposed when crude oil leaked out of a Union Oil well just off the coast of Santa Barbara, California. The slick would eventually cover 800 square miles (2,072 square km) of Pacific Ocean and wash up along 30 miles (48km) of the Southern California coastline. It took Union Oil workers 11 days to cap the well; in the meantime, nearly 4,000 birds died after they were coated with oil. Many dolphins died as well, their blowholes clogged with the oily sludge. By the time the well was finally capped, some 5,000 barrels of oil, or about 210,000 gallons (794,936L), had spewed out of the undersea well.

The spill prompted Congress to act. Months later, Congress passed the National Environmental Policy Act (NEPA), which requires federal agencies to monitor and regulate industrial projects believed to have a significant ecological impact. Even so, as Congress held hearings that year on the spill, lawmakers heard some unnerving predictions from experts. Said David K. Bickmore, an engineer employed by Santa Barbara County, "Representatives of the Union Oil Company have testified that no prudent engineer would guarantee that this tragic event won't be repeated. It is my considered opinion that they are right."[9]

> "Representatives of the Union Oil Company have testified that no prudent engineer would guarantee that this tragic event won't be repeated. It is my considered opinion that they are right."[9]
>
> — David K. Bickmore, an engineer commenting on the 1969 Santa Barbara oil spill.

Growth of an Industry

Despite the new rules imposed by Congress, the offshore drilling industry continued to grow. Today, about 2,900 active oil platforms operate across the globe, including more than 1,500 in U.S. waters.

Offshore oil reserves represent a significant portion of the energy output of other countries. Europe, Great Britain, and Norway produce nearly 2 billion barrels, or 84 billion gallons (318 billion L), of oil a year from North Sea platforms. In the Middle East, such oil producers as Saudi Arabia and the United Arab

Blowout Preventer

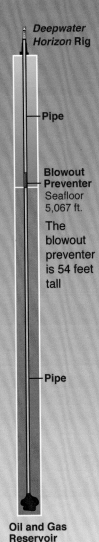

Deepwater Horizon Rig

Pipe

Blowout Preventer
Seafloor
5,067 ft.

The blowout preventer is 54 feet tall

Pipe

Oil and Gas Reservoir

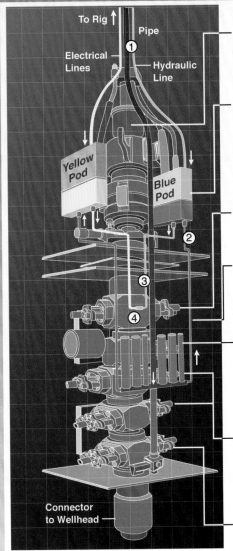

To Rig ↑
Pipe
Electrical Lines
Hydraulic Line
Yellow Pod
Blue Pod
Connector to Wellhead

Annular Preventers

Can create a seal around the drill pipe or seal off an open wellbore when there is no pipe.

Control Pods

Receive electrical signals from the rig and direct the movement of hydraulic fluid. Upper portion has electrical parts; the lower portion has hydraulic valves. Only one pod is activated at a time.

Blind Shear Ram

Cuts the drill pipe and completely seals the well.

Casing Shear Ram

Cuts drill pipe or casing in an emergency when the rig needs to disconnect from the well quickly.

Accumulators

Store fluid sent from the rig. During an emergency pressurized fluid from these canisters can provide force to power the blind shear ram.

Pipe Rams

Seal off the space between the outside of the drill pipe and the well bore and keep the pipe centered.

Test Ram

Used to test the rams above it.

What should happen in an emergency

1 In a blowout, a rig worker presses an emergency button. A signal is sent from the rig down an electrical line to one of the control pods.

2 The control pod directs hydraulic fluid from the rig and from a bank of pressurized canisters, called accumulators . . .

3 through a valve called a shuttle valve, and into the blind shear ram. Some blowout preventers have a separate emergency system with its own shuttle valve.

4 The blind shear ram cuts through the drill pipe and seals the well, preventing oil from gushing out.

Source: *New York Times*, "Investigating the Cause of the Deepwater Horizon Blowout," June 21, 2010. www.nytimes.com.

Emirates are known mostly for their desert-based oil fields, but those countries also maintain rigs in the Persian Gulf that produce nearly 1 billion barrels, or 42 billion gallons (159 billion L), of crude a year.

Indeed, new offshore discoveries are constantly being announced—in 2006 huge reserves were discovered offshore of the Cuban coastline—as much as 4.6 billion barrels of oil as well as 10 trillion cubic feet (0.3 trillion cubic m) of natural gas. That is enough oil and natural gas to fulfill Cuba's needs and even make

Ixtoc I and Union Oil: What Went Wrong?

The *Ixtoc I* and Union Oil blowouts occurred for vastly different reasons. In the case of the Union Oil blowout, investigators concluded that the drilling crew failed to sink casing far enough into the well to prevent the leak. Casing is metal tubing that lines the shaft of the mine below the ocean floor. At the Union Oil well, the casing was used for just 239 feet (73m) of the well's depth, even though the well had been drilled some 3,500 (1,067m) feet deep. Investigators speculated that oil rising in the unlined well seeped into natural fissures in the rock, finally bursting through the seafloor.

A much different engineering error caused the *Ixtoc I* blowout. Investigators concluded that the drilling crew failed to pump a sufficient amount of "mud" into the well. In the jargon of the offshore industry, mud is a heavy fluid used to lubricate the drill bit and clean the drilled rock out of the hole. Mud is also used to force the oil and gas to stay in the well, preventing the fuels from seeping out. During the drilling operation the crew detected that the mud pressure was low in the well, so the decision was made to withdraw the drill and temporarily cap the well. As the drill was being withdrawn, the oil and gas broke through the mud barrier and blew out the well.

the tiny nation into an oil exporter. "It's a very sizeable reserve that is well documented,"[10] says Jonathan Benjamin-Alvarado, a professor of political science at the University of Nebraska.

Of the offshore platforms in operation across the globe, about 400 are regarded as "deepwater" operations, meaning they sit atop 1,000 feet (305m) or more of water. About a third of the deepwater platforms are operating in the Gulf of Mexico. Because of the vast amounts of water beneath the deepwater platforms, most are not anchored to the bottom by fixed pillars—rather, they float on the surface as their flexible pipelines, tethered to the bottom by flexible cables that allow for little drift, draw oil out of the seabed.

The modern offshore oil industry was spawned from some very humble beginnings. On August 27, 1859, Edwin Drake, a former railroad conductor, drilled the first land-based oil well near Titusville, Pennsylvania. Oil oozed to the surface, where it was stored in wooden barrels. Although his methods were crude and his workers drilled just 70 feet (21.3m) down, virtually no difference exists between Drake's well and the wells that are today drilled thousands of feet below Earth's surface by the world's biggest oil companies.

Within three decades of Drake's strike, oil explorers had fanned out across the continent. Some found their way as far west as California, where rigs were set up on the beaches. In 1887 Californian Henry LaFayette Williams saw that some of the best producing wells were located nearest the surf. Williams erected a 300-foot-long pier (91.4m) from the beach of Summerland, California, and placed a drilling rig atop the wooden structure. When the well produced oil, other drillers rushed to sink their own wells along the coastline. Most of the wells were located within 1,200 feet (366m) of shore—all were placed atop piers similar to the structure built by Williams.

Thirst for Oil

By the early years of the twentieth century, the world had developed a true thirst for oil. In Detroit, Michigan, the Ford Motor Company revolutionized the mass production of automobiles and would churn out some 15 million cars by 1927. Ford's competitors added millions of more cars to the road. All were powered by the gasoline-fueled internal combustion engine. Meanwhile, ships converted from coal-powered steam engines to oil-burning engines, while furnaces that burned heating oil or natural gas were installed in homes, office buildings, and factories. The aviation industry also exploded in the twentieth century—all aircraft flown in the world today are completely dependent on oil-based fuels.

To meet this staggering need for oil, huge petroleum fields were established in Texas and Oklahoma as well as other places in America. Meanwhile, the oil fields in such Middle East countries as Saudi Arabia, Kuwait, and Iraq became the world's most important oil producers. Russia, Canada, and Venezuela have also emerged as major oil-producing countries.

Offshore operators were rushing to meet the need as well. In 1938 the first free-standing offshore rig was established in the Gulf of Mexico. The rig sat atop timber piles sunk into the seafloor. The rig stood in just 13 feet (4m) of water about a mile (1.6km) off the coast of Cameron, Louisiana, in the southwestern corner of the state. Nine years later, oil drillers established a platform 12 miles (19km) off the coast of Terrebonne Parish, Louisiana. This was the first rig established out of sight of land. Clearly, huge oil reserves were to be found in the Gulf of Mexico—by 1949, 44 drilling platforms were in operation in the gulf.

In 1969, workers clean up oil-drenched straw dumped on the beach in Santa Barbara, California, to soak up oil from a leaking drilling rig off the coast. The spill prompted passage of a law requiring federal monitoring and regulation of industrial projects that might damage the environment.

Drilling Deeper

In the six decades since Williams drilled for oil at the end of a 300-foot pier (91.4m), the offshore oil industry had established itself as an important component of America's energy infrastructure. It was helped along by Congress, which enacted legislation in 1953 opening the outer continental shelf, or OCS, to offshore drilling. The OCS is a sloping undersea plain that surrounds the continental United States and leads out to the deep ocean.

To get to the crude buried in the OCS, oil companies had to be willing to invest tens of millions of dollars in exploration as well as the development of the rigs and drilling equipment. It also meant they had to find ways to drill in deeper water. Indeed, they determined that off the coast of California, the OCS sloped steeply downward just a few miles out from shore.

The first attempts to pursue oil in the OCS were made not with drilling rigs mounted on platforms but on ships. The first of these ships, owned by a consortium of four oil companies, made its maiden voyage along the California OCS in 1953. To drill, the ship was anchored to the bottom by chains and cables. The ship, a mothballed U.S. Navy vessel, was named the *CUSS I*. (*CUSS* stood for the four oil companies that owned the ship, Conoco, Union, Shell, and Superior.) The *CUSS I* was able to drill in about 350 feet (107m) of water—a substantial depth at the time. The success of the *CUSS I* led to the development of the *CUSS II* in 1962. It was the first ship designed specifically as a floating oil-drilling barge. The *CUSS II* was twice the size of the *CUSS I* and able to drill in 600 feet (183m) of water.

By the mid-1960s, oil companies had developed platforms that could sit atop rigid pillars anchored to the bottom hundreds of feet below sea level. Other rigs were stationed atop floating platforms that could be towed from site to site by tugboats, then anchored to the bottom with flexible cables or other temporary means. These platforms were truly engineering marvels of the era. In 1965 *New York Times* journalist Werner Bamberger toured a platform in the Gulf of Mexico and reported, "In recent years these rigs have grown to mammoth proportions. One of them,

> "Considering the social and economic potential of the ocean, this country's oil industry cannot afford to remain becalmed by indifference."[12]
>
> — Charles F. Jones, Humble Oil president in 1965.

now under construction in Japan, measures 342 by 340 feet. And some of them can drill in 250 feet of water."[11]

The First Deepwater Well

By the late 1960s the fixed and floating platforms could sit atop as much as 600 feet (183m) of water, but they still were not getting to the richest deposits along the OCS, which were located at depths of 1,000 feet (305m) or more. At that time the oil company engineers had not yet devised the methods and infrastructure needed to drill to deepwater depths. Industry insiders knew very well, though, that the true riches in the sea were located further offshore at depths that were as yet unattainable. In 1965 one oil company executive, Humble Oil president Charles F. Jones, urged his industry onward when he said, "Considering the social and economic potential of the ocean, this country's oil industry cannot afford to remain becalmed by indifference."[12]

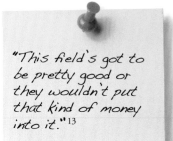

"This field's got to be pretty good or they wouldn't put that kind of money into it."[13]

— Frank White, head of the drilling crew aboard Shell Oil's Cognac Platform, erected in 1978.

Over the next decade, oil companies relentlessly pursued offshore oil reserves. Rigs were set up further and further off the coastlines and in deeper and deeper waters. Finally, in 1978 Shell Oil Company erected the Cognac Platform in the Gulf of Mexico near Morgan City, Louisiana. (Shell named the platform "Cognac"—after a French alcoholic beverage—as a tribute to the French influence in the region.) The platform stood 1,205 feet (367m) high; moreover, Cognac was perched atop rigid pillars in 1,025 feet (312m) of water.

Cognac was the first oil platform to sit atop more than 1,000 feet (305m) of seawater, making it the first true deepwater rig. Shell had good reason to pick the site near Morgan City—geologists had estimated that some 100 million barrels of oil as well as 500 billion cubic feet (14.2 billion cubic m) of natural gas were available beneath the seafloor. The cost of erecting the Cognac Platform was $800 million. "This field's got to be pretty good or they wouldn't put that kind of money into it,"[13] said Frank White, head of the drilling crew aboard Cognac.

Era of Environmental Activism

The achievements marked by the *CUSS* ships as well as the Cognac Platform illustrated that the 1960s and 1970s were part of an era

Henry LaFayette Williams and Summerland

The international offshore oil industry owes its founding to Henry LaFayette Williams, a former Union Army major who was a dedicated "Spiritualist," meaning he believed he could contact the dead through the medium of the séance. After the Civil War, Williams made his way to California where he bought a 1,000-acre ranch (405ha) overlooking the Pacific Ocean. He divided the ranch into small lots he hoped to sell to other Spiritualists.

He decided to name the new town "Summerland," which is a Spiritualist term for the afterlife. (Some California historians have also speculated that the name had a double meaning—that Williams also hoped to lure homesteaders looking for year-round pleasant weather.)

Soon after moving in, the earliest Summerland residents found natural gas leaking out of the ground. Further investigation found oil deposits as well. An oil boom soon invaded the town as speculators arrived with drilling equipment. After oil was discovered, Williams's dream of establishing a Spiritualist community fell by the wayside, particularly after he conceived the notion of drilling for oil from a pier he built 300 feet (91.4m) into the Pacific Ocean.

of dynamic and rapid growth in offshore oil production, but some looked upon these achievements with a sense of dread. During the late 1960s the environmental movement first found its voice. In 1966 Congress adopted the Endangered Species Preservation Act, providing protections for animals whose species are in danger of disappearing due to overhunting or urbanization of their habitats. (The fact that the national symbol of America, the bald eagle, was placed on the Endangered Species List helped dramatize the dire circumstances faced by many species.)

In 1968 two important books were published: *The Population Bomb*, which suggested that the environment of Earth could not sustain the growing human population, and the *Whole Earth Catalog*, which helped spark the movement to grow foods untouched by pesticides or chemical-based fertilizers. In 1969 activists started planning the first Earth Day—an annual national celebration devoted to protecting the environment.

Amid this growing interest in environmental activism, a blowout occurred at the Union Oil well near the Santa Barbara coastline. In Santa Barbara, as oil from the spill washed up on shore, environmental activists as well as town residents mobilized. They staged a public march to a wharf that oil companies utilized to ship supplies to their offshore rigs. In protest, the marchers blocked the entrance to the wharf and refused to leave. "We had the whole town riled up," says Bud Bottoms, a Santa Barbara resident. "We blocked [the wharf] with our bodies and these big trucks tried to come aboard and they backed off. Everybody felt like we'd done something."[14]

> *"There had been this assumption that [offshore drilling] would be safe because proponents of drilling and the [oil] companies had said it would be. Suddenly, the evidence was to the contrary."*[15]
>
> — Dennis Kelso, of the environmental group Ocean Conservancy, looking back on laws passed in the 1960s and 1970s.

Primary Mission

The demonstration was staged to get the attention of lawmakers in Washington, D.C., but, clearly, Congress was already paying attention. Months after the Union Oil spill, the Cuyahoga River in Cleveland, Ohio, caught fire due to the abundance of chemicals that were being dumped in the waterway by industries. In response to such ecological disasters as the Union Oil spill and the Cuyahoga River fire, Congress adopted the National Environmental Policy Act of 1969, giving the federal government wide-ranging powers to ensure the environment is protected against abuses by industry. Indeed, the act established protection of the environment as a primary mission of the U.S. government.

For the offshore oil drillers, the act meant that before they could sink a new well they had to show their plans to federal regulators, who could withhold approval should they suspect that the drilling project had the potential for damaging the environment. Says Dennis Kelso, vice president of the environmental group

Ocean Conservancy, "There had been this assumption that [offshore drilling] would be safe because proponents of drilling and the [oil] companies had said it would be. Suddenly, the evidence was to the contrary. So it directly influenced the public consciousness that contributed to major national environmental legislation."[15]

Moreover, throughout the 1970s Congress imposed additional regulations on the offshore oil industry. The Clean Air Act of 1970 required rig operators to report the amount of pollutants the drilling operations emit into the air. The Coastal Zone Management Act of 1972 gave state governments the right to challenge offshore drilling permits on environmental grounds. In 1973 Congress adopted a new Endangered Species Act; this measure imposed strict restrictions on offshore drilling operations that could affect endangered marine species. And in 1977 the Clean Water Act mandated that drilling operators maintain strict standards when discharging pollutants into the oceans.

The offshore industry did have a few friends in Congress: Many proponents of offshore drilling represented coastal states such as Louisiana where offshore oil drilling provided a significant boost to the local economy. "We have . . . oil wells off the coast of Louisiana, and we have been drilling out there for a quarter of a century," complained Louisiana senator J. Bennett Johnston in 1978. "The so-called danger from oil wells has simply not been proved, it has been disproved, and we need to get on with that drilling."[16]

> "The so-called danger from oil wells has simply not been proved, it has been disproved, and we need to get on with that drilling."[16]
>
> — J. Bennett Johnston, Louisiana senator in 1978.

Incident at *Ixtoc*

A year after Johnston made those remarks, the "so-called" danger of drilling in the Gulf of Mexico turned into a very real danger. On June 3, 1979, a well below the *Ixtoc I* drilling platform suffered a blowout. Located in the Bay of Campeche along the Yucatan Peninsula in Mexico, the well spewed more than 3 million barrels, or 140 million gallons (530 million L), of crude into the gulf, much of it washing onto Mexico's beaches. As with the Union Oil spill, the *Ixtoc I* incident caused severe environmental damage—the crude killed wildlife and fouled the Mexican coastline. *Ixtoc I* was not an American operation: It was owned by Pemex, the Mexican government–owned oil company.

Clean-up crews (right) spray chemical dispersant on spilled oil that surrounds the burning Ixtoc I *drilling platform after a 1979 blowout near Mexico's Yucatan peninsula. More than 140 million gallons of crude oil spewed into the Gulf of Mexico.*

The well may have been located well south of American waters, but it still caused environmental damage to the American coastline. Oil washed up along the Texas coastline some 600 miles (966km) from the well. Hit hard by the catastrophe was South Padre Island, a town on the southern tip of the 130-mile-long Padre Island (209km), which is located along the Texas coastline just north of the border with Mexico. Soon after the spill, "tar balls" started washing up on South Padre Island beaches as well as on beaches further north along the island. Tar balls are clumps of crude, some pea-sized, some larger. "What we have are multiple patches of oily substances, in different forms, stretching over some 400 miles or so in the gulf,"[17] reported Joseph L. Gibson, a U.S. Coast Guard official who monitored the *Ixtoc I* spill.

Much of the South Padre Island community was affected by the spill. South Padre Island is a resort town—soon after the tar balls started washing ashore, many tourists stopped visiting the beaches. Hotels had to endure cancellations during the summer of 1979, which should have been their busiest season. Moreover, shrimp fishing boats based on Padre Island faced restrictions that reduced their catches. Ken Walker, the manager of Callaway Seafoods, which operated seven shrimp boats out of the Padre Island harbor, likened the oil slick to a hurricane. "You never know where it's going to go or how bad it will be,"[18] he said.

Ixtoc I was not a deepwater well—the rig sat in just 150 feet (46m) of water, giving the repair crews easy access to the wellhead. Even so, Pemex engineers struggled with the leak as millions of gallons of oil spewed into the gulf. It took the engineers 10 months to finally staunch the flow.

Moratorium on Exploration

The incident at the *Ixtoc I* well had a vast impact on American offshore oil operations. When the *Ixtoc I* well started leaking oil, most of the OCS was still unexplored. At the time, virtually all drilling offshore of the American coast was confined to regions near Alaska, Southern California, and the western portion of the Gulf of Mexico. Drilling had not yet commenced in the eastern portion of the gulf or offshore of the entire Atlantic coastline, much of the Pacific coastline, and huge areas off the Alaskan coastline—particularly north of Alaska in the Beaufort and Chukchi seas.

In 1981 Congress banned further offshore exploration and drilling, confining the industry to the places where drilling was already established. Among those places are the western half of the Gulf of Mexico, adjacent to the Texas, Louisiana, and Mississippi coastlines. Near Alaska most drilling is confined to the Cook Inlet, which borders about 200 miles (322km) of Alaska's southern coastline. North of Alaska, small portions of the Chukchi and Beaufort seas are open to drilling, but the vast majority of those two immense seas remain closed to drilling. Finally, a handful of rigs are in operation off the California coast.

People along the California coastline, who had already lived through one spill and saw how another spill had fouled the Texas and Mexico coastlines, welcomed the moratorium. Environmentalists feared that another spill along the California coastline would be even harder to control, given the rough seas and swirling winds of the region that could possibly propel the slick over an area of hundreds of square miles.

Industry officials reacted harshly to the ban. "Offshore, the government is delaying the search for energy," complained Shell Oil vice president E.F. Loveland. "Ninety-six percent of our Outer Continental Shelf—96 percent—of that area is unexplored . . . the Eighties must be the decade of production, must be the decade in which we again find our bearings on energy."[19]

But the moratorium on new exploration remained in place until 2008 when Congress finally lifted the ban in response to skyrocketing oil prices. Even so, no exploration or new drilling in the outer continental shelf has occurred in the years following the congressional action. In 2010, less than a month after the Obama administration announced guidelines on where it would permit new offshore drilling in the OCS, the *Deepwater Horizon* ignited and collapsed into the sea, setting off an unprecedented ecological disaster. As Congress and the administration struggled with the harsh realities of offshore drilling, federal regulators refused to permit new exploration in the OCS.

Overshadowed by Danger

In the years since the *Ixtoc I* leak, the offshore oil industry has continued to perform incredible feats of engineering. In 2003 a ship owned by Chevron-Texaco set a world record for exploration by drilling a well while anchored atop more than 10,000 feet (3,048m) of water. A year later, a Shell Oil rig stationed on a floating platform drilled a well into the seafloor more than 7,500 feet (2,286m) below sea level. And yet, as the Union Oil, *Ixtoc I*, and *Deepwater Horizon* catastrophes illustrate, the impressive engineering accomplishments of the offshore oil industry are often overshadowed by the incredible dangers the wells pose to the environment.

Facts

- Texas oilman Louis Giliasso was first to mount an oil derrick onto a floating barge; in 1928 Giliasso had the barge towed into the Gulf of Mexico where it started drilling the same day it was anchored.

- Seven of the top 20 oil fields in U.S. waters are located in deep water.

- Oil companies operating in the Gulf of Mexico have found they have to move further and further offshore to find rich deposits. By 2011, 80 percent of the oil produced in the gulf will be pumped from platforms sitting atop 1,000 feet (305m) or more of water.

- Between 1993 and 2009 oil production in the Gulf of Mexico doubled from about 800,000 barrels a day to more than 1.6 million barrels per day.

- The cost of developing a well in 100 feet (30.5m) of water has been estimated at $100 million; the cost of developing a deepwater well has been estimated at $1 billion or more.

CHAPTER TWO

Is America's Energy Security Dependent on Offshore Oil?

In the early morning hours of October 6, 1973, Egyptian and Syrian armed forces launched a surprise attack on Israel, touching off what would become known as the Yom Kippur War. Within weeks, the Israelis were able to repel the attacks, thanks in large part to a huge airlift of arms and supplies provided by the U.S. government.

In the Middle East, Arab leaders reacted harshly to America's willingness to aid the Israelis. In a fit of anger, King Faisal of Saudi Arabia abruptly cut off his country's shipments of oil to the United States. Other Arab oil exporters followed the Saudis' lead and halted their exports as well. Said Saudi oil minister Sheikh Zaki Yamani, "Saudi Arabia, which has thrown all its weight in men and money into the battle against Israel, will not hesitate to use its oil, too."[20]

Virtually overnight, the price of gasoline more than doubled. American car owners found themselves waiting in long lines at the gasoline pumps as supplies ran thin. Industries reliant on oil slowed production. The American economy soon fell into a recession.

After six months, the Arab oil ministers lifted the embargo. In Washington, D.C., President Richard M. Nixon resolved to make it a national priority for America to become energy independent and, therefore, no longer reliant on unstable foreign powers for oil. Declared Nixon, "Let us set as our national goal . . . that by the end of this decade we will have developed the potential to meet our own energy needs without depending on any foreign energy source."[21]

What Is Energy Security?

Despite Nixon's pledge, the United States did not achieve energy independence by 1980. In fact, nearly four decades after the Arab oil embargo, America is still not energy independent. The United States imports 62 percent of its oil, and while many of the country's oil suppliers are on friendly terms with America (Saudi Arabia is now an American ally), some are not. Venezuela, for example, has maintained testy relations with the United States.

Angered by U.S. support for Israel, which was attacked by Egypt and Syria in 1973, Saudi Arabia abruptly halted U.S. oil shipments. This action sparked a gasoline shortage, resulting in long lines and limited supplies, as illustrated by this scene at a Pennsylvania gas station at the time.

To many experts, one way to help achieve energy security is to expand offshore oil exploration and production. Says Jack Gerard, president of the American Petroleum Institute (API), the trade association of American oil companies,

> We can produce at home more of the oil and gas we'll be consuming, including promising resources off our coasts, creating hundreds of thousands of jobs for Americans and returning many billions of dollars in desperately needed revenue to our government—or we can increase reliance on supplies produced outside the United States, depriving our nation of these benefits and weakening our energy security.[22]

A guaranteed and reliable source of energy is vital to the success of a modern society. Without energy, life would come to a virtual halt in America and other industrialized nations. Without fuel for cars and trucks, Americans would not be able to get to work or transport goods. Oil provides energy for many factories as well as the ingredients for plastics and other products. Aviation and marine fuels are refined from oil. The 1973 Arab oil embargo showed how even a partial disruption in the oil supply greatly disrupted life and harmed the American economy. Says Phillip E. Cornell, an energy consultant to the North Atlantic Treaty Organization, "The lack of sufficient energy provision to critical domestic networks or infrastructures can cause the breakdown of essential services from healthcare and safety systems to communication, transport, emergency response, and basic utilities."[23]

The Arab leaders who cut off the oil to America in 1973 were certainly aware that the embargo would cripple the American economy—they chose to use oil as a weapon. That threat has never gone away. In recent years, Venezuelan president Hugo Chavez has often punctuated his criticisms of the United States with threats to halt oil exports. In 2010, for example, Chavez warned American leaders to stay out of a dispute between Venezuela and neighboring Colombia,

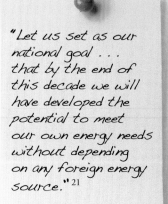

"Let us set as our national goal . . . that by the end of this decade we will have developed the potential to meet our own energy needs without depending on any foreign energy source."[21]

— Richard M. Nixon, president of the United States, 1973.

Norway's Offshore Oil Brings Energy Independence

The only country in the world that has managed to achieve energy independence through offshore drilling is Norway. Through its platforms in the North Sea, Norway produces more than 1.3 billion barrels of oil a year. With a population of less than 5 million—about 2 percent of the population of the United States—that is more than enough oil to sustain Norway's needs. Indeed, Norway's extensive offshore production has enabled the country to become the world's 10th largest oil exporter.

Former U.S. House Speaker Newt Gingrich, a proponent of offshore drilling, says Norway has been able to establish its offshore industry while still protecting its environment. "The truly remarkable fact is that Norway has built this robust offshore oil and gas drilling industry alongside large and thriving fishing and tourism industries," says Gingrich.

However, Norway may be facing an end to its years of energy independence as well as its status as an oil exporter. Energy Watch Group, which monitors worldwide energy consumption, estimates that oil reserves in the North Sea total about 19 billion barrels. Energy Watch Group predicts that by 2030 Norway's offshore production will drop to less than half of what it is today. Meanwhile, a study by Erasmus University in the Netherlands has predicted that the North Sea will run out of oil shortly after 2050.

Newt Gingrich, "Report from Norway: Why They Don't Have an Energy Crisis and We Do," *Human Events*, June 10, 2008. www.humanevents.com.

in which Colombian officials charged that Chavez had provided a safe haven to Colombian rebels. (The Marxist rebels aided by Chavez are believed to be financing their revolutionary activities through the drug trade; to combat the rebels' drug trafficking rings, Colombia has made use of U.S. financial aid and military advisers.) "If there is any armed aggression against Venezuela from Colombian territory or from anywhere else, promoted by the Yankee empire, we would suspend oil shipments to the United States,"[24] Chavez declared.

Affordable Energy

Energy security goes beyond the guarantee of a steady flow of oil—to be truly energy secure, the oil must be affordable. Because American industry is so heavily reliant on oil, if the fuel ever becomes prohibitively expensive the cost would have a devastating effect on the American economy. To achieve true energy security, a modern society must find a way to achieve energy independence: the ability to power all modes of transportation, all industries, homes, and other infrastructure with *affordable* energy generated totally at home or from reliable, friendly, and politically stable energy-producing nations.

Certainly, Venezuela does not qualify as reliable, friendly, or politically stable. Nor do some of the other providers of oil to America, such as Nigeria, Angola, and Iraq. Nevertheless, Venezuela provides Americans with more than 1 million barrels, or 42 million gallons (159 million L), of oil a day. That represents about 5 percent of the oil consumed by Americans each day. (Collectively, Nigeria, Angola, and Iraq supply about 1.5 million barrels a day to American consumers.)

If Chavez ever makes good on his promise to cut off oil to the United States, the sudden disruption in supply would impact the American economy. Indeed, a sudden cutoff of Venezuelan oil would drive up prices at the gas pumps and slow industrial production, both of which could help spark a recession and put Americans out of work.

Many Uses for Oil

Venezuela is among the four top foreign oil suppliers to the United States. Other top oil exporters to the U.S. include Canada, about 1.8 million barrels a day; Mexico, about 1.2 million barrels a day; and Saudi Arabia, about 1 million barrels a day. In fact, Americans import some 3.6 billion barrels of oil a year while drawing 2.2 billion barrels domestically in places like Texas, Oklahoma,

California, and Alaska as well as from offshore platforms. The off-shore platforms account for 27 percent of the oil produced in the United States, or about 594 million barrels a year.

That oil goes for many uses. A barrel of crude contains about 42 gallons (159L) of oil. A single barrel produces about 19.5 gallons (74L) of gasoline, 9.2 gallons (35L) of home heating oil, and 4.1 gallons (15.5L) of jet fuel. The rest is devoted to various other uses, including lubricants, kerosene, and oil used to repair and repave roads.

Oil Prices Spiral Upward

In 2008 a number of factors contributed to a sudden and steep rise in international oil prices. One major factor in the spiraling cost of oil was the emergence of China and India as major oil consumers. Each country sought to become international economic powers, and, therefore, their governments devoted huge resources to industrializing their economies. China and India both ramped up their need for oil. Between 2001 and 2007 China's consumption of oil rose by nearly 70 percent, from 4.5 million barrels a day to 7.5 million barrels per day, while India's consumption rose by about 30 percent, from 2.1 million barrels per day to 2.7 million barrels per day. With China and India demanding more oil, prices spiraled upward across the globe.

Other factors also contributed to the steep rise in prices. Nigeria, which is the fifth largest oil exporter to the United States, at some 600,000 barrels per day, went through a period of political turmoil, which temporarily disrupted the country's exports. That meant that from time to time in 2007 and 2008, less oil was on the market for sale, and therefore prices rose. Moreover, by the end of the 2000 decade, the European Union (EU) had emerged as a major international economic force. The 27 European countries in the EU use a common currency, the euro, which increased in value due to the economic power of the EU. As the euro gained strength, the ability of the American dollar to buy goods on the international market decreased. Therefore, American tourists visiting foreign countries found their money bought less. Americans doing business on an

"If there is any armed aggression against Venezuela from Colombian territory or from anywhere else, promoted by the Yankee empire, we would suspend oil shipments to the United States."[24]

— Hugo Chavez, president of Venezuela, 2010.

international basis found their money bought less as well—among them were American oil traders, who were forced to pay higher prices for a barrel of oil.

All these factors came together in 2008 to boost oil prices to record levels. In January 2007 the price for a barrel of oil on the international market stood at about $50. Eighteen months later, oil traders found themselves paying more than $145 a barrel. Those prices were reflected at the gasoline pumps; during the summer of 2008, the price for a gallon of gas hit more than $4 in many communities. Although the price of oil eventually dropped, the tremendous burden American consumers faced at the gas pump was one of the factors that helped push the U.S. economy into a recession in 2008.

"Drill, Baby, Drill"

As oil prices skyrocketed, President George W. Bush called for an end to the moratorium on outer continental shelf exploration and drilling. Congress responded by letting the OCS bans

U.S. drivers hoping to fill their gas tanks encountered huge price increases in 2008, as this gas station sign in Los Angeles shows. The unprecedented increases resulted from many factors including spiraling demand and political turmoil in other countries.

expire—although an immediate lifting of the moratorium would have no immediate effect on the nation's oil supply. Typically, it could take 10 years for an offshore rig to produce oil once exploration begins and a promising well is identified.

Moreover, a somewhat political element contributed to the sudden fervor in Washington for ending the OCS moratorium—2008 happened to be a presidential election year. Republican presidential candidate John McCain made expansion of offshore drilling a central issue in his campaign, advocating opening up more portions of the American coastline to exploration and drilling. ("Drill, baby, drill," became a popular slogan voiced by McCain's supporters.) "What we really need is to produce more, use less and find new sources of power," McCain declared during a campaign appearance. "The next president must be willing to break with the energy policies not just of the current administration, but the administrations that preceded it, and lead a great national campaign to achieve energy security for America."[25]

McCain's opponent, Barack Obama, acknowledged that he would not oppose expansion of offshore drilling, either. Obama won the election and, in March 2010, unveiled plans to open a wide swath of the outer continental shelf along the Atlantic coastline to offshore drilling. Also in the plan, huge expanses of the Chukchi and Beaufort seas were to be opened for exploration but not drilling at this time. Finally, a small expansion of drilling off the California coast was proposed. "We're here to talk about energy security," said the president. "The bottom line is this: Given our energy needs, in order to sustain economic growth and produce jobs, and keep our businesses competitive, we are going to need to harness traditional sources of fuel."[26]

> "What can we do to improve our energy security? A big part of the answer lies at home and off our shores and beneath our oceans."[27]
>
> — Randall Luthi, president of the National Ocean Industries Association, a trade association for the offshore oil industry, 2010.

Vast Oil Reserves Available

Experts generally agree that expansion of offshore oil production would increase the reserves available to energy companies, which, in turn, would help decrease America's dependence on foreign oil. Offshore of Alaska, portions of the Beaufort and Chukchi seas that have been proposed for exploration cover some 130 million acres (52.6 million ha). Nineteen billion barrels of oil are estimated to lie beneath the two seas. In addition, expanded exploration of Cook Inlet is expected to yield another billion barrels of oil. Geologists also believe that vast reserves remain untapped in the Gulf of Mexico. One 2003 study estimated that at least 60 billion barrels of oil can be extracted from a 9,500-square-mile region (24,605 square km) of the gulf that lies offshore of Texas, Louisiana, and Mississippi.

"What can we do to improve our energy security?" asks Randall Luthi, president of the National Ocean Industries Association, a trade association for the offshore oil industry. "A big part of the answer lies at home and off our shores and beneath our oceans. One of the greatest potential sources for domestic oil and natural gas, the outer continental shelf, remains largely unexplored and still 'off limits.'"[27]

Newt Gingrich, a former U.S. House speaker and possible candidate for president in 2012, advocates expanding exploration and drilling in the OCS. He contends that this action would help ensure that the United States would not find itself at the mercy of its enemies for oil. "The worldwide demand for energy will continue to rise, resulting in ever higher energy prices and more money filling the coffers of [hostile] oil-producing states," says Gingrich.

> There is only one solution for reversing this dynamic: increase American production. The first steps to expanded production are to change the law to allow more oil and gas development offshore and in Alaska. . . . With increased American oil production, world oil prices will also be restrained by our declining demand for imported oil. This will curtail the huge influx of money currently pouring into oil producing rogue states.[28]

Support for Drilling Dwindles

Less than a month after Obama announced the plan, the *Deepwater Horizon* exploded in flames and collapsed into the gulf while, a mile below, millions of gallons of crude oil started spewing into

The Africa Command

The western coast of Africa from Morocco to Angola is home to some of the most promising offshore oil fields in the world. For example, off the coast of Ghana, the Jubilee Field is expected to yield some 1.2 billion barrels of oil. That field has drawn interest from such oil companies as ExxonMobil, BP, and Chevron. Moreover, offshore wells along the Angola coast are already producing nearly 500 million barrels a year.

The richness of the African offshore oil reserves, and their value to America, prompted the U.S. military to establish the Africa Command, or AFRICOM, in 2007. A primary mission of AFRICOM is to protect the offshore platforms from attacks by pirates, terrorists, or other insurgents.

In recent years, the United States has become more reliant on oil from Africa. The United States now imports 21 percent of its oil supply from African countries, which provide supplies from both onshore and offshore fields. That number is expected to grow to 25 percent by 2015. "There's a steady flow of African countries that are exploring [for oil]," says Emira Woods, codirector of Foreign Policy in Focus, a Washington, D.C.–based organization that studies international energy issues. According to Woods, the United States has recognized the importance of providing a military presence along the western coast of Africa to protect those offshore oil fields.

Quoted in Lawrence Delevingne, "Critics Target U.S. Military Command," Inter Press Services News Agency, June 2, 2008. http://ipsnews.net.

the environment. Public opinion, which had favored expansion of offshore oil production during the presidential campaign, suddenly turned sharply against further offshore exploration and drilling. One poll, take by CBS News, showed that before the *Deepwater Horizon* spill, 64 percent of Americans favored new exploration and drilling in the OCS. In the weeks following the incident, though, support among Americans for expanded offshore drilling had fallen to just 46 percent in favor. Meanwhile, the poll also showed that following the massive spill in the gulf, 41 percent of Americans believed that offshore drilling is too risky to expand. Before the accident, just 28 percent of Americans held that view.

The expansion of offshore production outlined by Obama had been included in a 2010 comprehensive energy bill that would have also enacted a tax on industries that continued to rely heavily on fossil fuels, which include oil, natural gas and coal. The program was designed to reduce America's reliance on fossil fuels, both from an energy security standpoint as well as in the interest of reducing the emissions of greenhouse gases into the atmosphere, which many scientists believe are at the root of climate change.

The bill died in the Senate. Some senators feared that placing constraints on the use of fossil fuels would hamper American industries and limit their growth. Meanwhile, many senators could not agree to expand offshore oil exploration and drilling in the wake of the *Deepwater Horizon* crisis. A typical response to the spill was offered by Senators Frank Lautenberg and Robert Menendez as well as Representatives Frank Pallone and Rush Holt, all of New Jersey, who issued a joint message to President Obama that said:

> In the wake of the tragic accident, loss of life, and pollution in the Gulf of Mexico from the *Deepwater Horizon* oil rig, we are even more steadfastly opposed to any offshore drilling that could imperil the environment or economy of coastal New Jersey. While we appreciate the White House's announcement that no additional offshore drilling will be authorized until a full investigation of the accident is complete, we urge you to go further and reverse your decision on proposed new offshore oil and gas drilling for the outer continental shelf.[29]

Pushing for Clean Energy

During his March 2010 news conference announcing expansion of the OCS to exploration and drilling, the president made it clear that as new oil reserves are identified, the country would also move toward development of such renewable resources as solar, wind, and geothermal power. Said Obama administration spokesperson Robert Burton, "I would say that this comprehensive approach is a lot less 'drill, baby, drill,' and more 'drill where it's responsible, promote efficiency, invest in clean energy and create jobs in the future.'"[30]

Many American environmental leaders believe that the U.S. government should not pursue further development of offshore resources and instead concentrate fully on developing renewable resources. They argue that encouraging homeowners and businesses to convert to renewable sources of energy would help reduce greenhouse gas emissions as well as enhance energy security because Americans would rely on less imported oil. "Oil and gas development will only further stress and rapidly increase the effects of climate change on this fragile marine Arctic ecosystem which is already experiencing significant challenges from the rapid pace of global warming,"[31] said Nicole Whittington-Evans, acting director of the Alaska regional office of the environmental group Wilderness Society.

In recent years the federal government and many state governments have adopted measures to enhance development of alternative energy sources. Many states have mandated that utilities make some of their electricity through solar and other renewable resources. Rhode Island, for example, has mandated that utilities operating in the state must make 16 percent of their power through alternative sources by 2020. Meanwhile, the federal government has given homeowners and businesses generous tax incentives to convert to renewable resources, while some states provide grants to people to help them pay for alternative energy systems.

These are the types of activities that advocates for clean energy insist the government should be pursuing—rather than finding new places to drill in the OCS. "It makes no sense to threaten the East Coast of America with spills and other drilling disasters when we're about to unleash the real solutions to energy dependence—cleaner cars, cleaner fuels, and clean energy,"[32] says Doug O'Malley, field director for the environmental group Environment New Jersey.

"When Brazil discovered huge new offshore oil reserves, it caused a national celebration. It was a matter of pride. When we discover oil here . . . it's treated as a matter of shame."[34]

— U.S. Representative Jeb Hensarling of Texas.

U.S. Senators Byron Dorgan of North Dakota and George Voinovich of Ohio argue that renewable resources are directly tied to enhancing America's energy security. "As long as we are largely dependent on foreign oil to transport goods, services and people, we remain vulnerable to economic and geopolitical threats to our nation's security," the senators write. "The ultimate goal is to power our cars with domestically produced electricity that can be produced from a range of resources. This energy would not be subject to the whims of terrorists and hostile regimes."[33]

Risky Path

Despite efforts to convert the nation's energy infrastructure to renewable resources, many believe that offshore oil drilling should remain an integral component of America's energy supply. Representative Jeb Hensarling of Texas says, "When Brazil discovered huge new offshore oil reserves, it caused a national celebration. It was a matter of pride. When we discover oil here . . . it's treated as a matter of shame."[34] And Representative Duncan Hunter of California, a steadfast supporter of expanding offshore oil production, posted this message on his campaign Web site: "The only way to free ourselves from terrorist despots who negotiate international policy using oil prices is to keep working on alternative energy while at the same time following an 'all of the above' approach. We must build more oil refineries, build nuclear facilities, and drill."[35]

Nevertheless, as crews struggled to clean up the mess in the Gulf of Mexico, prospects for expanding offshore drilling in the OCS remained as murky as ever. Given the heightened public opposition to offshore drilling, political leaders may be less inclined to endorse new exploration and drilling along America's coastlines or repeal the long-standing moratorium on expanded drilling in the OCS. In the meantime, many experts predict fossil fuel use will continue to rise. Even with the expansion of solar, wind, and other renewable resources, the U.S. Energy Information Administration predicts that the United States will still import half of its oil by 2035 and fossil fuels will make up nearly 80 percent of the energy used by Americans.

Such statistics would seem to indicate that Americans have some difficult choices ahead as they strive for energy security. To meet future demand, a search for new offshore oil reserves may be necessary. As the *Deepwater Horizon* incident illustrates, though, the path toward energy independence can be risky and unpopular.

Facts

- The recent industrialization of the Chinese economy boosted the country from its status as the fourth largest oil consumer in 2001 to second largest in 2007; the United States remains the world's largest consumer of oil.

- The United States buys 90 percent of the oil that Venezuela produces; therefore President Hugo Chavez is unlikely to cut off oil sales to America.

- New drilling in the outer continental shelf is expected to have little impact on the price of gasoline at the pump—by 2030 gasoline prices would drop by less than 3 cents a gallon even if the reserves prove particularly fruitful.

- Under President Barack Obama's proposal to open the Atlantic coast to offshore exploration, some 167 million acres (67.6 million ha) of ocean, from the northern tip of Delaware to the central coast of Florida, would be open for drilling.

- More than 10 billion barrels of oil are estimated to be available in the outer continental shelf along the West Coast of the United States.

- According to Next Era Energy, a Florida-based electric power company, enough sunlight strikes an 8,100-square-mile region (20,979 square km) of the Mojave Desert each year to meet the electricity demand for the entire country.

CHAPTER THREE

Can the Environment Recover from Offshore Drilling Accidents?

In 1969 a barge transporting oil struck some rocks off the coast of West Falmouth, Massachusetts, dumping nearly 200,000 gallons (757,082L) of its cargo into the sea. Soon, the oil washed up on shore.

More than 40 years later, scientists continue to find lingering effects of the spill in the ecology of the West Falmouth shoreline. In one 2007 experiment, marine biologist Chris Reddy examined the habits of fiddler crabs. He found them acting as though they were drunk. The crabs would traipse over the sand erratically, and the critters did not do a good job of hiding from predators. Moreover, fiddler crabs normally dig burrows into the sand, which play an important role in helping the marsh grasses grow—their burrows provide paths for oxygen to infiltrate the grass roots. But the fiddler crabs in West Falmouth were digging far fewer burrows, and Reddy observed that the grass was suffering.

Scientists believe the oil from the barge spill has remained in the environment after more than four decades. It has fouled the ecosystem of the shoreline and is consumed by the wildlife, including the fiddler crabs, which are affected both physically and cognitively by the oil. Indeed, the West Falmouth case illustrates how toxins from an oil spill can start a disastrous chain reaction: The fiddler crabs, affected by the oil, have been digging fewer burrows that provide oxygen for the marsh grass. As a result, the marsh grass recedes. Other wildlife that live in the marsh grass, such as dragonflies, mosquitoes, and other insects, disappear as well, meaning birds have less food. Seeking food, the birds go elsewhere.

During a visit to the shore in 2010, Reddy extracted a clump of marsh grass from the sandy beach and sniffed the roots. He could detect a distinct, oily aroma. "This taught us oil doesn't always go away,"[36] he said.

Initial Damage Severe

Many oil spills have occurred over the past few decades—not only from offshore oil rig blowouts but also from shipping accidents and similar mishaps. Therefore, scientists have had many opportunities to study the ecosystems of the regions affected by the spills. In many cases, as in West Falmouth, the effects linger for decades. In other cases, scientists have been stunned at how well the environment has recovered. Indeed, some scientists believe that due to the unique ecology of the Gulf of Mexico, the effects of the *Deepwater Horizon* accident may not be as dire as environmentalists have predicted. Says Jeffrey W. Short, a scientist who has studied the effects of the *Exxon Valdez* tanker spill in Alaska, "Thoughts that this is going to kill the Gulf of Mexico are just wild overreactions. It's going to go away, the oil is. It's not going to last forever."[37]

Regardless of how well the environment recovers, the initial damage is often severe. The oil spilled from the *Exxon Valdez* washed up along 1,200 miles (1,931km) of Alaskan coastline. More than 10,000 volunteers flocked to the scene, and many were filmed by TV cameras scrubbing gooey black oil from birds and other wildlife. Although the response was swift, the environmental damage was severe: At least 250,000 birds are estimated to have died from the effects of the spill. The death toll also includes nearly 3,000 sea otters as well as 300 seals. "It's pathetic," said marine biologist Rick Steiner, who surveyed the damage caused by the *Exxon Valdez* spill in 1989. "There are dead otters and others dying, pumping their way out of the water and it looked like a few dead sea lions were floating in the water. There were bald eagles feeding on dead sea birds. It was a field day for the eagles but I think they're going to pay for it soon."[38]

More than two decades after the *Exxon Valdez* spill, oil remains in the environment of Prince William Sound. Indeed, recent tests conducted in Prince William Sound found that the livers of ducks and sea otters indicate they are still ingesting oil. According to Short, some of the oil from the tanker spill seeped deep down into the beaches and may still be found there a century from now.

Danger to the Wetlands

In the wake of the *Deepwater Horizon* spill, scientists believe that if any portion of the Gulf of Mexico is likely to suffer for generations to come, it would be the wetlands of the coastal states. As the term suggests, wetlands are areas of the environment that are permanently saturated with water. They are marshy areas that spawn many varieties of plant and animal life. Wetlands are also very sensitive to encroachment by development. Many state and local communities strictly regulate the amount and nature of development that may occur near wetlands, fearing that heavy construction can disrupt the sensitive ecosystems of the marshy areas.

In the aftermath of the *Deepwater Horizon* explosion, many photos emerged depicting oil coating the plant life of the Louisiana wetlands. Because of past spills, scientists believe they can predict how the wetlands of the coastal states would be affected by the *Deepwater Horizon* blowout. For example, five years after the West Falmouth spill, another barge struck rocks along the Massachusetts coastline, dumping as much as 370,000 gallons (1.4 million L) of oil into the ocean. The oil washed ashore near the town of Winsor Cove, coating marshy grasslands similar to those found in Louisiana.

The specific species of marsh grass affected by the spill is known as spartina. After just a few months, the spartina along the coast had virtually disappeared. "The first year, it was just like

Oil Spill Threatens Marine Ecosystems in the Gulf of Mexico

The Gulf of Mexico, one of the largest U.S. areas for offshore drilling, is home to one of the world's most productive fisheries and a variety of marine and plant life. The April 2010 oil spill threatens the Gulf's fragile marine ecosystem.

Major wildlife habitats

Kemp's Ridley Sea Turtles — Sea birds — Grass — Mangroves — Fish — Shellfish

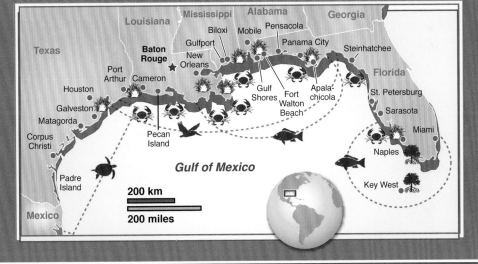

Source: McClatchy DC, "A Vast Marine Nursery," May 5, 2010. http://media.mcclatchydc.com.

a moonscape,"[39] says marine biologist George Hampson, who inspected the spartina following the accident.

The loss of the marsh grass would cause other environmental damage. Without the spartina to stabilize the soil, the Winsor Cove wetlands started eroding, washing away into the Atlantic surf. After a few years, six feet (2m) of shoreline had disappeared. Hampson has returned many times to Winsor Cove to inspect the area hit by the spill. "I'd say the grasses are just beginning to grow back,"[40] he says.

What Caused the Oil Plume?

Four months after the *Deepwater Horizon* spill, scientists detected evidence of a vast oil plume, measuring some 22 miles (35.4km) in length, that formed about 3,000 to 4,000 feet (914m to 1,219m) below the surface. A study by the Woods Hole Oceanographic Institution in Massachusetts suggested that the use of chemical dispersants to break up the oil caused the formation of the plume—driving the oil below the surface.

Faced with the ugly prospect of 210 million gallons (795 million L) of sludge washing up on the Gulf Coast beaches and marshlands, the U.S. Coast Guard agreed to let BP break up the oil by using the dispersants. It was believed that by breaking up the oil into microscopic particles, tiny microbes would consume the oil, thus ridding the gulf of most of the sludge.

Instead, when the oil was broken up into tiny particles it sank below the surface, where microbes are less active. Instead of floating on the warm surface of the Gulf of Mexico, the oil sank to a depth where the water is about 40°F (4.4°C). Richard Camilli, chief author of the study for Woods Hole, says the oil has been preserved in the gulf just as food is preserved in a refrigerator. "In colder environments, microbes operate more slowly," says Camilli. "That's why we have refrigerators."

Quoted in Seth Borenstein, "A 22-Mile Oil Plume Is Deep in Cold Gulf," *Philadelphia Inquirer*, August 20, 2010.

Waterproof and Warm

When the oil coated the wetlands of the Gulf Coast, it came into contact with the animals as well. When animals are exposed to oil, the first parts of their bodies to be affected are their feathers and fur. Feathers help keep birds waterproof and warm. In mammals, fur helps trap air near the animal's body, creating a natural insulating barrier between the animal's skin and the environment.

When birds and land animals are coated with oil, they lose their natural insulation that keeps them warm. In addition, when the oil coats feathers and fur, the animals lose their ability to swim or otherwise move through the water. That is why so many sea otters died in the *Exxon Valdez* spill: These mammals, ordinarily very at home in the water, suddenly found themselves without their natural buoyancy. Birds whose feathers are coated with oil cannot fly. When such creatures cannot swim or fly, they are unable to look for food. Many die of starvation.

A big danger to the animals occurs when they ingest the oil. Mammals and birds coated with oil will attempt to clean themselves. When they lick their fur with their tongues or peck at their feathers with their beaks, the animals ingest the oil. Crude oil contains hundreds of chemicals, many of which are toxic. Among them are benzene, which can kill white blood cells and damage the body's natural immunity; toluene, which can cause kidney damage; and xylene, which can impede the growth of young animals.

Other chemicals contained in crude oil are known as polycyclic aromatic hydrocarbons (PAHs). These chemicals are believed to be capable of causing cancer, mutations, and birth defects. Following the *Deepwater Horizon* spill, scientists were particularly concerned about birds picking up oil on their bodies, then flying back to their nests. There the oil would be transferred to the birds' eggs or young hatchlings, killing them in the process. "Many of our worst fears are coming true," says Cornell University ornithologist Ken Rosenberg. "No bird that depends on oil-impacted wetlands or water is going to be completely safe."[41]

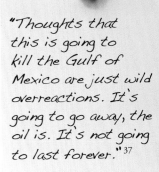

"Thoughts that this is going to kill the Gulf of Mexico are just wild overreactions. It's going to go away, the oil is. It's not going to last forever."[37]

— Jeffrey W. Short, scientist, commenting on the effects of the BP spill.

Underwater Plume

The dangers from oil spills can also be found away from shore. Fish swimming through the oil slick can ingest the harmful chemicals through their gills. The oil will also deprive the water of its oxygen, which fish take in through their gills. In the *Deepwater Horizon* spill, fish were believed to have died when the oil stuck to their gills, making it impossible for them to take in oxygen.

Other marine life can be impacted as well. For example, sea turtles were particularly affected by the *Deepwater Horizon* spill.

As the turtles paddled to the surface to draw air into their lungs, the oil coated their eyes and noses. Many turtles ingested the oil as well. Moreover, the thick crude simply made it more difficult to swim. Wildlife biologists believe many sea turtles died from exhaustion as they wore themselves out struggling to swim through the heavy crude. "It is the very lucky turtle that is picked up and brought to us," said John Hewitt, who headed a turtle rescue program in the Gulf of Mexico for the Audubon Aquarium of the Americas in Louisiana. "One can only imagine the numbers of turtles floating around in the oil."[42]

As the oil gushed out of the well and into the gulf waters, much of the slick was visible on the surface as a ruddy crude. Hundreds of miles of booms, which are hollow plastic tubes, were laid across the coastline to corral the slick. Thousands of boats were enlisted and deployed to skim the oil off the surface. The U.S. Coast Guard also oversaw several controlled burns in which the oil in the water was ignited. After four months of such efforts, the U.S. Coast Guard declared that cleanup crews had captured and removed nearly 75 percent of the oil.

However, scientists soon discovered an underwater plume of oil that proved to be of much more concern than the sludge on the surface. The plume endangered marine life—the fish, turtles, jellyfish, and sperm whales swimming through the plume ingested the toxins. Four months after the spill, and one month after the well was capped, a study by the Woods Hole Oceanographic Institution in Massachusetts suggested the oil plume was 22 miles (35.4km) in length and that it sat some 3,000 to 4,000 feet (914m to 1,219m) below the surface of the gulf. "Where has all the oil gone?" asks marine scientist Chuck Hopkins of the University of Georgia. "It hasn't gone anywhere. It still lurks in the deep."[43]

The plume is also expected to affect the food chain. Plankton found deep below the surface were coated with oil from the plume, which was ingested by tiny fish. Those small fish were consumed by larger fish, and so on. "The organisms most likely to be harmed by the oil plume are those at the base of the food chain,"[44] says Andrew Juhl, a Columbia University marine biologist.

"Where has all the oil gone? It hasn't gone anywhere. It still lurks in the deep."[43]

— Chuck Hopkins, marine scientist, University of Georgia, in aftermath of BP spill.

More Harm than Good

Scientists believe the plume may have been caused by the use of chemical dispersants during the cleanup operation. As oil spewed into the gulf, BP was permitted by the Coast Guard to employ chemicals to break up the slick so that the oil formed into microscopic particles. These particles are then consumed by bacteria living in the ocean. During the cleanup, BP sprayed more than a million gallons (3.8 million L) of dispersants on the gulf waters.

Some scientists believe the dispersants may have caused more harm than good. The dispersed oil tends to drop lower into the ocean where it could be consumed by marine life, thus adding new toxins to the food chain.

The use of dispersants is only one activity of the cleanup that concerns scientists. As BP workers traipsed along beaches and waded through wetlands, they were eager to shovel oily clumps of sand and soil into plastic bags. Clearly, though, as the cleanup workers

A brown pelican, weighed down by oil, lifts its wings but goes nowhere in this scene photographed along the Louisiana coast almost two months after the BP spill. Unable to fly and search for food, this bird and others whose wings are coated with oil will likely die.

turned over shovelful after shovelful, they were disturbing the natural habitats of the plant and animal life in the gulf. Scientists say they are anxious to avoid the effects of a cleanup of a tanker spill that fouled the coastline of northwestern France in 1978. That year the tanker *Amoco Cadiz*, caught in gale winds, struck the rocky coastline, spilling some 67 million gallons (353.6 million L) of oil.

The French cleanup workers acted swiftly—perhaps too swiftly. The French moved in with bulldozers and tractors, determined to scoop up the oil before it had a chance to seep into the environment. In scooping up the oil, though, the heavy equipment tore apart great swaths of coastland, sacrificing many healthy stretches of marshes in the interest of capturing the oil. Today, the region of the *Amoco Cadiz* spill is still missing some 40 percent of its native vegetation. "In the case of the *Amoco Cadiz*, the cleanup operations were more deadly than the pollution itself,"[45] says Jean-Claude Dauvin, a University of Lille marine biologist.

Hands Across the Sand

Following the *Deepwater Horizon* spill, as BP deployed thousands of workers to clean up the beaches and wetlands of the gulf, environmental activists mobilized as well. Many organized "Hands Across the Sand" demonstrations, in which hundreds of activists linked hands along the beaches to protest offshore oil drilling. A national Hands Across the Sand event was staged on June 26, 2010. On that day, more than 900 protests were organized, mostly on beaches along the Gulf Coast, but organizers in some 20 other countries staged events as well.

At a demonstration in Jupiter, Florida, Greg Lyon, head of a Florida chapter of the national environmental group Surfrider Foundation, said, "The oil spill is a crisis and a wake-up call that we're the ones paying the price of offshore drilling."[46] More than 750 people participated in the Jupiter protest. Meanwhile, in Seaside, Florida, protester Jimmy Green said, "The one avenue that is available to the people is to protest."[47]

And in Jacksonville Beach, Florida, the protest started silently—hundreds of demonstrators started the event by holding hands and standing quietly. After about 15 minutes, the protest-

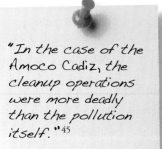

"In the case of the Amoco Cadiz, the cleanup operations were more deadly than the pollution itself."[45]

— Jean-Claude Dauvin, University of Lille marine biologist.

ers started chanting "No Drill, No Spill!" over and over again. "I'm tired of looking at the news and feeling helpless," said protester Trevor Brandl. "This is letting those in power know that no one industry should be able to put an entire coastal economy and coastal environment at risk."[48]

The protesters along the American beaches were joined by protesters in other countries. Many demonstrated against the *Deepwater Horizon* spill, but many voiced concerns about offshore drilling operations closer to home. A few weeks after the Hands Across the Sand event, activists in Germany staged a demonstration in front of the headquarters for the country's economic ministry to demand the German government oppose new oil exploration in the North Sea. To punctuate their message, the demonstrators doused themselves with thick brown paint to illustrate the environmental damage that an oil spill could cause. "Germany is a member of an international convention to protect the seas and the Northeast Atlantic Ocean," insisted one of the activists, Juergen Knirsch. "[Germany] must demand a ban . . . with the goal to stop deep sea drilling in the Northeast Atlantic."[49]

Protests against offshore drilling even reached as far away as Thailand. On the Thai coastal island of Koh Samui, protesters staged their own version of Hands Across the Sand when thousands linked arms to demonstrate against an oil company's plans to explore about 26 miles (42km) off the coast in the Gulf of Thailand. Participants in the protest included environmental activists as well as students, employees of hotels and other tourism-related industries, and fishermen who feared their livelihoods would be endangered should oil spill into the gulf.

Evolving Microbes

Despite the fears expressed by the environmental activists, many scientists believe the ecology of the Gulf Coast will recover. Most do not expect an overnight recovery. Thirty years after the offshore *Ixtoc I* blowout, scientists are still inspecting the coastline of the Bay of Campeche in Mexico—and they continue to find evidence of the spill. In 2010 two biologists, Wes Tunnell of Texas A&M University and Julio Sánchez of Universidad Autónoma of

"The oil spill is a crisis and a wake-up call that we're the ones paying the price of offshore drilling."[46]

— Greg Lyon, Florida chapter of the Surfrider Foundation on the impact of the BP spill.

Oil: Hazardous to Humans, Too

To help encourage tourists to return to the Gulf of Mexico following the *Deepwater Horizon* spill, President Barack Obama and his nine-year-old daughter Sasha went for a swim in the gulf in Saint Andrew Bay near Panama City, Florida. St. Andrew Bay is more than 300 miles (483km) from the site of the *Deepwater Horizon* spill and, therefore, health officials believe the Obamas were in little danger of coming into contact with tar balls or other remnants of the spill.

Others who come into close contact with the oil, particularly those hired to clean it up, may experience health effects. Following the *Exxon Valdez* spill in 1989, more than 1,800 cleanup workers complained about such ailments as respiratory problems and skin irritations. In 1993, after the tanker *MV Braer* spilled 26 million gallons (98.4 million L) of crude off the coast of Scotland, cleanup workers reported a high incidence of headaches, throat irritations, skin irritations, and itchy eyes.

Psychological damage may have occurred as well. Following the *Exxon Valdez* spill, studies showed that people whose livelihoods were affected by the spill, mostly commercial fishermen, experienced periods of depression. "There were increased rates of drinking, drug use, fighting among friends and declines in social relationships," says Lawrence Paklinkas of the University of Southern California.

Quoted in Fred Tasker and Laura Figueroa, "Medical Experts Study Human Health Effects of BP Oil Spill in the Gulf of Mexico," *Miami Herald*, June 26, 2010. www.miamiherald.com.

Campeche, inspected a grove of mangrove trees along the coast. They found the mangrove trees to be growing in thinner numbers than is normal for the species. Also, when the two scientists dug into the soil they could detect an aroma of oil. "It smells like a newly paved road,"[50] says Sánchez.

And yet, Tunnell has examined the effects of the *Ixtoc I* blowout for much of his professional life and has been awed by the recuperative powers of the gulf. Tunnell and other scientists believe that the natural ecosystem of the gulf contains petroleum. There is so much oil beneath the seabed that it constantly seeps into the gulf through natural fissures in the ocean floor. Scientists suspect that the gulf environment has spawned resilient microbes that have adapted to the oil and are able to break it down as food. Says Tunnell, "Thirty years ago, that 140 million gallons of oil went somewhere. The gulf recovered and became very productive again. My concern is: Is it as resilient today as it was 30 years ago?"[51]

Uncertainty Lingers

Some preliminary evidence suggests the gulf is still very resilient. A month after the BP well was capped, scientists inspected the marshes of Barataria Bay, which is located in Louisiana some 40 miles (64km) from the site of the *Deepwater Horizon* spill. Soon after oil started oozing, it washed up along the wetlands of the bay. The oil immediately killed marsh grasses, mango trees, and other plant life. The inspection revealed, though, that some of the marsh grasses had started to return. "The marsh is coming back, sprigs are popping up,"[52] says Alexander S. Kolker a geologist with the Louisiana Universities Marine Consortium.

Other experts are not as sure. Monty Graham, a scientist at the Dauphin Island Sea Laboratory in Alabama, says he is concerned about the oil plume sitting below sea level. According to the Woods Hole study, the plume is likely to endure for many months and perhaps even several years. "We absolutely should be concerned that this material is drifting around for who knows how long," says Graham. "More likely, we'll be able to track this stuff for years."[53]

It would seem, then, that many scientists are unsure about the extent of the environmental damage caused by the *Deepwater Horizon* spill. If past spills such as those that affected Prince William Sound, West Falmouth, and Winsor Cove offer any clues, then chances are the environment of the Gulf Coast will continue to suffer for many years. Still, other scientists are confident the Gulf

> "Thirty years ago, that 140 million gallons of oil went somewhere. The gulf recovered and became very productive again."[51]
>
> — Wes Tunnell, Texas A&M University scientist who has studied the 1979 *Ixtoc I* spill.

Coast can bounce back and that nature has proven to be very resilient, even when faced with an unprecedented spill of 210 million gallons (795 million L) of oil.

Facts

- The 22-mile oil plume (35.4km) detected by scientists in the Gulf of Mexico is made up of dispersed microscopic particles and is therefore invisible to the naked eye; scientists discovered the plume through a chemical analysis of the water.

- About 40 percent of plankton studied near the *Deepwater Horizon* spill was found to have absorbed toxic chemicals from oil.

- During the first two months of the *Deepwater Horizon* cleanup, nearly a dozen oil spill workers were hospitalized with symptoms of nausea, dizziness, and chest pains.

- An active ingredient of the chemical dispersant used to break up the oil in the Gulf of Mexico is 2-butoxyethanol, which has been pinpointed as a cause of lingering health problems experienced by workers who helped clean up the *Exxon Valdez* spill.

- Tar balls from the *Deepwater Horizon* spill washed up on the beaches of Texas, Louisiana, Mississippi, Alabama, and Florida—all five states that border the Gulf of Mexico.

- A 2001 study of Prince William Sound in Alaska found oil from the *Exxon Valdez* remaining in the sand of more than half of 91 beaches surveyed.

- Three coral reefs in the vicinity of the *Deepwater Horizon* spill are believed to have been affected by the oil; a 2007 study found that when oil comes into contact with coral, reefs could take as long as 20 years to recover.

CHAPTER FOUR

Do the Economic Benefits of Offshore Drilling Outweigh the Risks?

As environmentalists gathered on the beaches of the Gulf Coast during the summer of 2010 to protest offshore drilling, a much different demonstration was being organized elsewhere in the region. In Lafayette, Louisiana, thousands of people filled a football stadium to stage a pro-drilling rally. Led by Louisiana Governor Bobby Jindal, the speakers denounced the Obama administration's decision to impose a temporary moratorium on exploratory offshore drilling.

The moratorium, which ended six months after it was imposed, did not affect wells already producing oil. The federal order halted work on just 33 exploratory rigs, many of them in deep water. The administration imposed the moratorium to determine whether any of the exploratory wells could suffer blowouts similar to the incident that sparked the *Deepwater Horizon* disaster. In lifting the moratorium, officials said they were satisfied that new drilling rules imposed after the spill would help prevent similar disasters in the future.

Speakers at the pro-drilling rally did not appreciate the president's efforts. Even though the action was taken to ensure that no other exploratory wells in the gulf would suffer massive leaks, opponents of the moratorium were more concerned with the short-term effects of the moratorium: that it could temporarily put some rig workers out of work while also impacting the local economies of the Gulf Coast. During the rally, they criticized the president and other federal officials for imposing the ban, fearing that even a modest halt to drilling would result in devastating economic consequences for Louisiana as well as other states where offshore drilling is big business. "We are in a war to defend our way of life," complained Jindal. "We will win this war. We shouldn't have to fight our own federal government. Just as we're fighting [the *Deepwater Horizon*] disaster, we're fighting another disaster caused by Washington, D.C."[54]

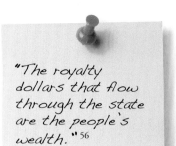

"The royalty dollars that flow through the state are the people's wealth."[56]

— Sean Parnell, governor of Alaska, speaking in 2008 on Alaska oil income.

On a street corner outside the stadium, a dozen protesters gathered to voice their opinions as well. They did not support the speakers inside the stadium; rather, they favored the moratorium. Lafayette resident Wallace Senegal held up a sign that read "We Support Wildlife and Fisheries." He said, "Let's quit blaming President Obama for this oil spill. He's looking out for our safety."[55]

Lucrative Oil Leases

Lafayette is a city of about 110,000, located some 40 miles (64.4km) from the Louisiana coastline. Many of the city's residents work in the oil and gas drilling industries. Among the residents of Lafayette are between 6,000 and 8,000 people who work on the offshore Louisiana platforms. Other residents are employed in support industries, from cargo workers who ship supplies to the offshore rigs to helicopter pilots who ferry busy executives to the platforms to refinery workers who turn the crude into gasoline, kerosene, and other petroleum products. An estimated 320,000 residents of Louisiana owe their jobs to offshore drilling. These workers pay local and state taxes and contribute to the economies of their hometowns and cities by shopping in local stores and eating in local restaurants. Overall, the offshore oil and gas industry contributes an estimated $30 billion a year to the Louisiana economy.

Even people who have no connection to the offshore industry benefit from the drilling platforms in the Gulf of Mexico as well as the rigs located off the coast of Alaska and elsewhere. Offshore oil drilling is not only enormously lucrative for the companies that find and sell the oil but also for the coastal states and the U.S. government as well. The reason: To get to the oil and gas, the drillers must lease the ocean floor and pay royalties to the owners—in this case, the state and federal governments.

Pain for Pensioners

The economic pain caused by the *Deepwater Horizon* spill was felt across the Atlantic Ocean by many retirees in Great Britain. As the spill worsened and BP was forced to invest billions of dollars in the cleanup, investors started doubting the health of the British-based company.

Fearing the company's collapse, many investors sold their BP stock, which drove down the overall value of the company. Before the spill, BP—one of the world's largest companies—was valued at more than $200 billion. A month after the spill, the stock sale had driven down the worth of the company by half.

Many retirees in Great Britain own BP stock. With the company's value cut in half, the value of their retirement savings had been reduced as well.

Many British officials called for calm and urged American political leaders to tone down their rhetoric about BP to help stabilize the market for the company's stock. "I would like to see a bit of cool heads rather than endlessly buck-passing and name-calling," said London Mayor Boris Johnson. "When you consider the huge exposure of British pension funds to BP, it starts to become a matter of national concern if a great British company is being continually beaten up on the airwaves."

Quoted in Jane Wardell, "As BP Sinks, Britons Worry," *Philadelphia Inquirer*, June 11, 2010.

In most cases, when oil is discovered on land the oil company will sign a lease with the landowner, who grants the company permission to erect a derrick and drill. Essentially, the oil company must pay rent to the landowner for use of the property. If oil is discovered, the landowner is entitled to a royalty—a percentage of the profits from the sale of the oil. Under law, landowners are granted mineral rights for whatever is found beneath the soil on their properties—whether it is gold, silver, coal, oil, or natural gas.

Most oil companies pay the landowners royalties of 12.5 percent, although for some very lucrative wells royalties could rise to as much as 25 percent of the value of the oil. Since many wells produce millions of barrels or more, the owner of land where a lucrative oil well has been found can become very wealthy.

Windfall Profits

When oil is found offshore, no private owners control the mineral rights. Under U.S. law, the coastal states own the mineral rights up to about 3.5 miles (5.6km) from their shorelines—although some states, including Florida and Texas, have won exemptions giving them rights as far as 10.5 miles (17km) from shore. Beyond the 3.5-mile barrier (5.6km) (10.5 miles [17km] in the case of Florida and Texas), the United States government controls the mineral rights—up to a distance of 230 miles (370km) from the coastline. This distance was negotiated under the terms of an international treaty.

It means that oil companies pay billions of dollars a year in lease payments and royalties to the coastal states as well as the federal government. Among the biggest winners are the states of the Gulf Coast—particularly Louisiana. The state earns more than $1.5 billion a year in revenue from the oil and gas industry. This is money the state uses to provide services to the taxpayers—the oil industry's money is used to help build and repair roads, maintain police departments and prisons, provide social workers to handicapped people, and finance a multitude of other services. If Louisiana and the other states did not receive the revenue from offshore oil leases and royalties, state lawmakers would be faced with the prospect of either cutting back services or raising taxes.

Some states have found ways to earn even more money from the oil industry. In 2007 lawmakers in Alaska imposed a separate tax on the profits of oil produced in the state. The so-called "windfall profits tax" covers revenue earned by the oil companies for their onshore as well as offshore production. In the first year of collections, Alaska earned $6 billion from the tax—that money was in addition to the lease fees and royalties paid by the oil companies for drilling on state-owned land as well as for offshore operations located within the 3.5-mile offshore zone (5.6km). Those royalties earned Alaska another $4 billion.

In fact, Alaska earned so much money from the oil industry, through the windfall profits tax as well as through lease and royalty income, that state lawmakers have decided to distribute it to Alaskans. In 2008 the state government sent payments of nearly $3,300 to every citizen of the state. Similar payments have also been made in other years. Says Alaska governor Sean Parnell, "The royalty dollars that flow through the state are the people's wealth."[56]

"We need the oil industry, and down here, there are only two industries— fishing and oil."[57]

— Devlin Roussel, Louisiana charter boat captain, in aftermath of *Deepwater Horizon* spill.

Staying Loyal to Oil

With profits such as those rolling into government coffers as well as the pockets of individuals, the fact that many of the residents and business owners of the Gulf Coast rallied around the offshore oil industry in the weeks following the *Deepwater Horizon* spill should not have come as a shock. Indeed, as Louisianans watched the sludge from the *Deepwater Horizon* accident foul their beaches and wetlands, many remained vehemently opposed to the Obama administration's moratorium that slowed oil exploration. Even Devlin Roussel, a charter boat captain, defended the oil industry. Roussel earns his living ferrying sport fishermen into the gulf, but due to the massive oil slick his boat spent many months stuck in port. "We need the oil industry, and down here, there are only two industries—fishing and oil,"[57] Roussel says.

Some 13,000 commercial fishermen are based in Louisiana. Many of them were idle throughout much of the summer of 2010 until the U.S. National Oceanographic and Atmospheric Administration declared the gulf waters safe for commercial fishing. In fact, shortly after the blowout the agency closed a third of the massive gulf to commercial fishing.

Oil discolors the water as it washes ashore on Grand Isle, Louisiana, shortly after the BP spill. Despite the sludge that fouled their beaches and wetlands, many Louisiana residents oppose efforts to stop or slow oil exploration in the Gulf of Mexico because of the jobs and business the industry provides.

According to the Louisiana Seafood Promotion and Marketing Board, which promotes Louisiana seafood, most local fishermen opposed the temporary moratorium even though another spill could have kept them idle for months more. "I am not in favor of the moratorium," said Harlon Pearce, chairman of the Louisiana Seafood Promotion and Marketing Board and the owner of a seafood processing company based near New Orleans. "You've got to be down here to see and feel what I'm telling you. It's our brothers, uncles, and cousins that are working in the oil industry."[58]

During the summer of 2010, businesses like those owned by Pearce suffered because the catch was much thinner than in prior summers. According to the Seafood Promotion and Marketing Board, the crab catch was down by 40 percent, while the shrimp harvest fell two-thirds below normal. As a result, many of the Louisiana seafood processing plants were forced to lay off workers. At AmeriPure, an oyster processing company in Franklin, Louisiana,

company officials were forced to lay off nearly 50 workers because of the poor harvest. And yet, many employees at AmeriPure stayed loyal to the oil industry. "Louisiana, we're known for our seafood and culture and stuff, but it's really an oil state,"[59] said Pat Fahey, co-owner of AmeriPure.

Higher Prices at Home

While no one questions that the Gulf Coast relies heavily on the offshore oil industry for jobs and other economic benefits, the *Deepwater Horizon* accident illustrates how offshore oil can also endanger jobs and the local economy should disaster strike. Following the blowout, the environmental damage caused by the leak fouled the gulf for months, greatly reducing such important Gulf Coast industries as commercial fishing and tourism.

During the summer of 2010, companies like those owned by Pearce and Fahey were forced to pay 20 percent above the average wholesale prices for seafood—an economic reality that occurs when prices rise due to scarcity of product. That price increase was eventually felt by people who live thousands of miles away from the Gulf of Mexico.

Overall, Louisiana fishing boats catch about 2 percent of the domestic seafood consumed in the United States. However, the Gulf of Mexico is the source of most of the shrimp and oysters consumed by Americans. In 2008 shrimp caught in the gulf made up 73 percent of the domestic catch, while gulf oysters made up 67 percent of the total domestic catch.

During the summer of 2010, many of the Louisiana shrimp and oyster boats remained moored in their harbors. Many were also enlisted by BP to help in the cleanup operation, either laying boom or skimming oil off the surface. (Regardless of their roles in the cleanup, if they were working for BP they were not catching fish.)

With the Louisiana boats catching less fish, supermarkets and restaurants in places like New York, Boston, Chicago, and Los Angeles had to pay higher prices for seafood as well. Restaurateur Jeff Tunks, who owns five New Orleans–style seafood restaurants in the Washington, D.C., area, said he was forced to

"*The industrial character of offshore oil and gas development is often at odds with the existing economic base of the affected coast communities, many of which rely on tourism, coastal recreation and fishing. If there's one spill or one disaster, the Outer Banks could be devastated for a long time.*"[63]

— Carolyn McCormick, Outer Banks Visitors Bureau in North Carolina, in 2009 testimony before congressional committee.

No Pain at the Pump

BP lost 210 million gallons (795 million L), or about 5 million barrels, of oil in the *Deepwater Horizon* spill. That may seem like a lot of oil but it is, in reality, little more than a drop in the ocean.

Americans burn through 5.8 billion barrels of oil a year, which means the loss in the gulf represented a tiny fraction of the oil Americans use. As such, oil industry experts believe the spill had no effect on the prices for gasoline Americans pay at the pump. "I don't think from a supply standpoint [the spill] will have any impact on prices," says Ben Brockwell, director of data pricing for the Oil Price Information Service, which tracks international oil prices. "There's plenty of crude around."

The *Deepwater Horizon* platform was erected over a region of the gulf known as the Macondo Prospect. BP owns the rights to the oil in the Macondo field. Reserves in the Macondo Prospect are estimated at between 50 million and 100 million barrels of oil. Following the *Deepwater Horizon* blowout, BP sealed the troubled well but indicated that at some point in the future it may drill again nearby, therefore providing oil from the Macondo Prospect to the American supply.

Quoted in Betsy Schiffman, "Gas Prices Creep Up After the Spill, Despite Weak Demand," *Daily Finance*, May 3, 2010. www.dailyfinance.com.

place $3 per meal surcharges on all his dishes. "It's unfortunate for us, a bleaker picture than we thought," Tunks said. "We have to figure out how much people are willing to pay for some of these things we've taken for granted for so long."[60] Elsewhere, many restaurants were forced to hike their prices for oysters and shrimp by 30 percent until supplies caught up with demand. Some restaurants stopped relying on the gulf to produce seafood and instead elected to obtain shrimp and oysters from other parts of the country.

Gulf Tourism Suffers

As the fishing industry felt the pain of the *Deepwater Horizon* blowout, leaders of the tourist industry near the Gulf of Mexico also felt economic stress during the summer of 2010. Tourism in the Gulf Coast states fell sharply after the *Deepwater Horizon* accident—even in places hundreds of miles away from the spill that were by no means tainted by tar balls. And tourism along the Gulf Coast rivals offshore oil in importance; an estimated 400,000 people work in tourism-related industries along the coast. In Louisiana alone, tourism generates $5 billion for the state's economy.

In Mississippi, officials estimated that tourism dropped by 20 percent in the months following the blowout of the BP well. According to Rick Forte, manager of the Beauvoir estate—the seaside home of Confederate president Jefferson Davis in Biloxi, Mississippi—the estate usually receives as many as 200 visitors a day. Following the blowout, Forte said, on some days just a handful of tourists visited the Davis home.

Forte pointed out that the *Deepwater Horizon* accident was the third severe blow to tourism in Biloxi since 2005. The others were Hurricane Katrina, which devastated parts of Louisiana and Mississippi in 2005, and the economic recession that started in 2008 and continued into 2010. "We had Katrina, then the recession, and now we have oil," said Forte. "It's hard to overcome this when no one is coming."[61]

Some areas of the Gulf Coast suffered even more. Hotel room bookings in the Miami, Florida, area dropped 30 percent following the *Deepwater Horizon* accident. On Dauphin Island, a coastal island near Alabama known for its beaches of white sands and exotic species of birds, hotel bookings dropped by 90 percent in the weeks following the blowout.

Moreover, while the shrimp and oyster fishermen were eventually allowed to return to their hunting grounds in the gulf, convincing tourists to come back may prove to be very difficult. Geoff Freeman, executive vice president of the U.S. Travel Association, a trade group, said it could take years before tourists start accepting

"While both the Exxon Valdez and Cosco Busan were spills from ships, not rigs, it does point out the danger caused by oil to the marine environment."[64]

— W.F. Grader Jr., Pacific Coast Federation of Fishermen's Associations, in 2009 testimony before congressional committee.

the Gulf of Mexico as a place to spend their vacations. "Once perceptions are formed, they take quite some time to change,"[62] says Freeman. One study commissioned by the U.S. Travel Association estimated that due to the oil spill, tourism-related industries along the Gulf Coast could lose as much as $22.7 billion by 2013.

Wiping Out Tourism Overnight

Given those types of potential losses, businesses based far away from the gulf fear similar consequences should offshore drilling be expanded into their home regions. For example, tourism officials have harbored concerns about opening the outer continental shelf to expanded oil and gas drilling. Carolyn McCormick, managing director of the Outer Banks Visitors Bureau in North Carolina, says the Outer Banks region of the state contributes $1 billion a year to the North Carolina economy, employing some 20,000 people in tourism and related businesses.

According to McCormick, one significant oil spill off the coast of North Carolina could wipe out Outer Banks tourism overnight. "The industrial character of offshore oil and gas development is often at odds with the existing economic base of the affected coast communities, many of which rely on tourism, coastal recreation and fishing," she says. "If there's one spill or one disaster, the Outer Banks could be devastated for a long time."[63]

Well before the *Deepwater Horizon* blowout, California fishermen were on record opposing the expansion of drilling along the California coastline. Many remember how the Santa Barbara spill of 1969 disrupted the commercial fishing industry in Southern California, even though that blowout was capped after just 11 days. Moreover, W.F. Grader Jr., executive director of the trade group Pacific Coast Federation of Fishermen's Associations, points out that the herring colonies of Prince William Sound have still not recovered more than 20 years after the *Exxon Valdez* spill.

In addition, Grader says, a relatively "minor" spill of just 58,000 gallons (219,554L) of oil from the tanker *Cosco Busan* also affected marine life. The spill, which occurred in 2007, was caused when the tanker struck a bridge in San Francisco Bay. The oil washed up

"You turn on the television and see the enormous disaster, and you say to yourself, 'Why would we want to take on that kind of risk?' "[65]

— Arnold Schwarzenegger, governor of California, commenting on debate over expanded oil drilling along California coast.

along 200 miles (322km) of California coastline and is believed to have killed many fish that would have otherwise been caught by commercial fishermen. "While both the *Exxon Valdez* and *Cosco Busan* were spills from ships, not rigs, it does point out the danger caused by oil to the marine environment,"[64] Grader says.

Some state officials have weighed the environmental and economic dangers of offshore drilling against the value of oil leases and royalties and have concluded that they are better off without more offshore drilling near their coastlines. In California, for example, expanding offshore drilling could add an estimated $7.4 billion to state coffers over the next 30 years, but Governor Arnold Schwarzenegger says that following the *Deepwater Horizon* incident he could not support an expansion of drilling along his state's coastline. Says the governor, "You turn on the television and see the enormous disaster, and you say to yourself, 'Why would we want to take on that kind of risk?'"[65]

Spills Are Rare

Despite the misgivings of officials such as Schwarzenegger, industry officials insist that oil spills—certainly those caused by offshore rigs—are still rare. In fact, according to the American Petroleum

Unable to continue shrimping operations in the oil-contaminated Gulf, shrimpers help with oil skimming efforts along the Louisiana coastline. Other boats remained moored in their harbors for several months after the spill.

Institute, oil and gas drilling is one of the safest industries in the world today. "Protecting the environment is a national imperative and oil and natural gas operations have established an impressive record of protecting our coastal waters," the API says in a statement. "The record also demonstrates that the U.S. offshore oil and gas industry is operating safely. . . . The offshore industry—despite the challenging environment and complex equipment involved— is safer than many other industries."[66]

Since 1969, during more than four decades of drilling for oil, just five major leaks from offshore rigs have occurred. They include the Santa Barbara, *Ixtoc I,* and *Deepwater Horizon* spills. Others include a 2009 spill off the coast of Australia, in which the well leaked 2,000 barrels a day before it was capped after two months, and a spill in 1983 in the Persian Gulf in which an Iranian rig leaked some 733,000 barrels before it was finally capped after two years. (It took the Iranians that long to cap the well because the platform was under constant attack by the Iraqi air force; at the time, Iraq and Iran were at war.)

Since the Santa Barbara spill, oil companies have developed better technology to help them protect the environment. They have used satellite imagery to help them track the oil slicks. Oil companies have also made use of better containment booms to help corral the crude. Also, better skimming technology has been developed to help crews remove the crude from the surface. "Offshore drilling is the safest way to go," says Roland Guidry, oil spill coordinator in the Louisiana governor's office. "Those guys don't spill oil."[67]

Benefits and Drawbacks

And yet, the *Deepwater Horizon* spill unquestionably caused havoc in the economies of the gulf states and even with segments of the American economy. Gulf seafood certainly became more expensive in the months after the spill. Meanwhile, hotel owners saw tourists flee the Gulf Coast. On the other hand, the revenue from oil leases and royalties has improved the lives of people who reside in Louisiana and Alaska; the offshore industry has provided jobs and has helped keep their taxes low. Perhaps the people who can best judge whether the economic benefits of offshore drilling outweigh the risks are those who live closest to the rigs.

Facts

- Two months before the *Deepwater Horizon* spill, Gulf of Mexico shrimp sold for $3.50 a pound; two months after the spill, with gulf shrimp in short supply, the price had more than doubled to $7.50 a pound.

- A study by Louisiana State University says the Obama administration's moratorium on exploratory drilling in the Gulf of Mexico temporarily put 8,100 oil rig workers out of their jobs.

- The 1989 *Exxon Valdez* spill is estimated to have cost the Alaska economy $300 million, most of which was in reduced incomes for more than 32,000 people who worked in commercial fishing in Alaska.

- A year after the *Exxon Valdez* spill, tourism in Alaska dropped by 8 percent.

- The oil industry and commercial fishermen in the Gulf of Mexico have maintained a long and friendly relationship: As far back as the 1930s, Texas oil prospectors hired fishing boat captains to help them find offshore pools of crude oil.

- Following the *Deepwater Horizon* spill, BP provided $25 million to Florida and $15 million each to Louisiana, Alabama, and Mississippi to help those states promote tourism; however, a study commissioned by the U.S. Travel Association says a $500 million promotional campaign is needed to lure tourists back to the gulf.

- In 2009 BP earned a profit of $16 billion.

CHAPTER FIVE

Can Offshore Drilling Be Made Safer?

T he disaster that caused the collapse of the *Deepwater Horizon* and subsequent oil spill in the Gulf of Mexico may have had its roots in one of the oil industry's most impressive achievements: In 1994 Shell Oil Company unveiled its $1.2 billion Auger deepwater drilling platform in the gulf. Sitting atop 2,800 feet (853m) of water, the Auger was the first of the "tension leg" oil platforms, tethered to the ocean floor by long flexible cables.

The Auger was among a new generation of deepwater rigs, using revolutionary techniques for anchoring the platforms and drilling wells. Industry leaders and others found themselves in awe of the Auger platform. "Auger is a state-of-the-art, deluxe marvel of engineering," said journalist Helen Thorpe, who visited Auger in 1996. "The platform is the size of two football fields, and I could feel it swaying back and forth."[68] Below Auger, eight wells drew oil from the seafloor. Leading down to the wellheads from the platform were long, flexible tubes that provided conduits for the oil to the surface. To allow for drift and strong ocean currents, the tubes could expand and contract like accordions.

At the U.S. Minerals Management Service (MMS), the federal agency charged with regulating the offshore oil industry, officials had a much different reaction to the Auger platform: They realized that the technology of offshore drilling was moving swiftly and that the laws giving them the authority to inspect the rigs and drilling equipment were probably outdated. The laws regulating offshore drilling were prompted by the Santa Barbara spill of 1969 and, therefore, mostly written by Congress in the 1970s—a time when the typical offshore platform sat atop just 700 feet (213m) of water. By the time the Auger started drilling, oil companies were using techniques and equipment that were not covered by existing law.

At the time the Auger platform went into operation, the prevailing attitude among lawmakers in Washington was not directed toward finding new ways to regulate the industry but instead centered on enabling the industry to operate unfettered by government interference. Says Chris Oynes, at the time a high-ranking official of the MMS, "It created a tone of 'Why should we try to have an aggressive program of regulations?'"[69]

Rush to Drill

Since the original post–Santa Barbara rules were written, Congress has not reexamined the laws that regulate offshore drilling. Instead of reviewing and updating the safety regulations, Congress looked for ways to promote offshore oil exploration. During the 1990s, with oil prices dropping and the economies of the oil-producing states faltering, Congress agreed to accept less money in mineral royalties on federal lands as well as offshore areas in order to spur exploration and development of new wells. This promise of enhanced profits prompted an intense rush by oil companies to find new places to drill in the gulf. In 1997 alone, the MMS approved more than 1,000 new oil leases in the Gulf of Mexico.

"I thought we had done a pretty good job of addressing the challenges that come with deep water. My opinion has not changed."[71]

— Chris Oynes, former official of the U.S. Minerals Management Service, commenting on quality of MMS work in wake of BP spill.

With so much activity occurring so quickly, and technology advancing so rapidly, the responsibility for ensuring that offshore oil drilling was being conducted safely fell not within the purview of government officials but with the executives and technicians of the oil industry. Says University of Houston professor Tyler Priest, who has studied the offshore oil industry, "It's not [that] they weren't worried by this, everyone in the industry knew that there were big challenges. I would say most major operators and contractors felt they were minimizing those risks, that they had a handle on it."[70]

Increased Scrutiny of Minerals Management Service

In the weeks following the *Deepwater Horizon* collapse, the MMS fell under heavy criticism from Congress as well as officials of the Obama administration, which blamed the agency for performing shoddy inspections on the rig. Specifically, the MMS failed to detect the deficiencies in the blowout preventer, which was unable to staunch the leak after the platform erupted in flames.

Moreover, the agency was criticized for maintaining a cozy relationship with the industry it was supposed to be regulating; MMS employees were known to accept gifts and free travel from oil companies. Also, over the years many MMS employees had accepted jobs in the oil industry, suggesting a conflict of interest at the MMS. After all, if MMS workers had their eyes on lucrative jobs in the oil industry, they might be more willing to look the other way when oil companies cut corners or otherwise ignored safety regulations.

MMS officials protested that they did the best job they could under the circumstances—that they lacked sufficient personnel to police the more than 1,500 offshore platforms operating in the gulf as well as along the California and Alaska coastlines. Given the constraints that had been placed on the agency, Oynes says, "I thought we had done a pretty good job of addressing the challenges that come with deep water. My opinion has not changed."[71]

No More Waivers

Other federal officials disagreed with Oynes's assessment. One month after the *Deepwater Horizon* disaster, the U.S. Interior Department announced that it had dissolved the MMS and created a new agency with new powers to police the offshore industry. Known as the U.S. Bureau of Ocean Energy Management, Regulation and Enforcement (BOEMRE), Interior Department officials said they hoped the agency's increased oversight of the oil industry would help avoid another offshore catastrophe. Said Michael Bromwich, a former U.S. Justice Department attorney appointed director of the BOEMRE, "The BP oil spill has underscored the need for stronger oversight of offshore oil and gas operations, more tools and resourc-

Containing Future Spills

After the blowout preventer on the *Deepwater Horizon* failed, BP tried several jury-rigged devices in its attempts to cap the well. Finally, after 85 days, a cap was fashioned to fit over the gushing pipeline; it was put in place by robot submersible vessels.

Given the repeated failures by BP to cap the well, offshore industry officials announced a $1 billion program to develop equipment that can be deployed rapidly to the scene of a deepwater blowout. The oil companies Exxon-Mobil, Chevron, ConocoPhillips, and Royal Dutch Shell each committed $250 million to the effort.

The four oil companies said they pooled the talents of some 40 engineers, who developed designs for caps and pipelines that can be deployed 10,000 feet (3,048m) below the surface and are capable of diverting up to 100,000 barrels of oil a day. "This is a risk-management gap we need to fill in order for the government and the public to be confident to allow us to get back to work," says Rex Tillerson, chairman of ExxonMobil.

To manage the program, the four oil companies created a nonprofit corporation, the Marine Well Containment Company, which will develop and deploy the system should it ever be needed. "One thing that has become clear is that we need to have a system that is flexible, adaptable and available for rapid response," says Sara Ortwein, ExxonMobil vice president for engineering.

Quoted in Jad Mouawad, "Four Oil Firms Commit $1 Billion for Gulf Rapid-Response Plan," *New York Times*, July 21, 2010.

es for aggressive enforcement, and a more effective structure for the agency that holds companies accountable. We will move quickly and responsibly on our reforms."[72]

In the future, the likelihood is that rig operators will have to undergo more stringent training and certification, and tough new inspection standards will be implemented. Indeed, the Interior Department has plans to hire hundreds of new offshore rig inspectors for the revamped agency.

Another change will be an end to so-called "environmental exemptions" that have been routinely granted to oil companies. Under the National Environmental Policy Act, which was adopted in the wake of the 1969 Santa Barbara spill, all projects that are believed to impact the ecology must be assessed by federal agencies for their environmental impacts. However, Congress left a loophole in the law, giving federal agencies the authority to waive the environmental assessments on a case by case basis. As lawmakers looked into the history of the law's enforcement, they found that many offshore drilling operations had routinely received waivers. Among the projects that were granted waivers is the *Deepwater Horizon*.

New Regulations Spark Industry Concerns

New regulations will also give the BOEMRE more time to review offshore drilling permits. The old regulations gave the MMS just 30 days to review a drilling permit. With so little time to examine the proposed drilling operations, the MMS is believed to have left many defects in the drilling plans undetected.

Offshore oil industry officials fear the new regulations will slow exploration and drilling. They predict the federal government will impose restrictive regulations on offshore drilling similar to those imposed on the nuclear power industry in the wake of the 1979 accident at the Three Mile Island nuclear power plant near Harrisburg, Pennsylvania. In that accident, mechanical failures and human errors led to a partial meltdown of the nuclear reactor core in the plant's Unit 2. Catastrophe was avoided when engineers managed to cool the core; if they had failed, the nuclear material could have melted through a concrete containment vessel, possibly igniting a devastating explosion.

Following the accident, the U.S. Nuclear Regulatory Commission imposed strict new regulations and inspections on the nuclear power industry. Those regulations are regarded as the main reason no new plans for nuclear power plants were approved for nearly 30 years. Says Bruce H. Vincent, chairman of the trade group Independent Petroleum Association of America, "Let's hope [the *Deepwater Horizon*] is not our Three Mile Island."[73]

The Blowout Preventer

As offshore oil industry leaders fear too much government regulation, many industry observers believe that more than enhanced oversight may be needed to ensure that accidents like the *Deepwater Horizon* do not happen again. For starters, they believe the blowout preventer may have to be re-engineered to ensure that the next time a mishap occurs, the failsafe device will react properly and seal the well.

Since the accident occurred, government investigators have focused their probe on why the oil suddenly gushed out of the wellhead and why the blowout preventer failed to staunch the flow. Although investigators expect it could take years to uncover the truth—after all, much of the evidence lies on the ocean floor, a mile beneath the sea—they believe the problems below the *Deepwater Horizon* started as rig workers began capping the well. The *Deepwater Horizon* was a drilling rig. After striking oil and establishing the well, rig workers started making the well ready for a handoff to another floating rig that would actually draw the oil from below the sea floor.

"Of particular concern is the ability to stop a blowout once it has begun."[75]
— U.S. Minerals Management Service, report issued in 2000.

To seal the well, cement was poured down the shaft. This is the point at which the calamitous events may have started. Investigators believe the cement did not properly seal the well; instead, it pushed a huge volume of natural gas upward through the 3.5-mile-long column (5.6km) leading from the reservoir of oil below the sea floor to the *Deepwater Horizon* platform. (In such reservoirs, natural gas can typically be found mixed with the oil.) The natural gas forced its way through the column, breaking through a barrier of heavy drilling mud, typically used to seal off the column. Pushing through the last layer of mud, the natural gas emerged at the top of the column, ignited, and destroyed the drilling platform, taking 11 lives.

Deficiencies in the Blowout Preventer

Throughout the drilling operation, a blowout preventer sat just above the sea floor at the wellhead. The blowout preventer is a

Blind Shear Ram

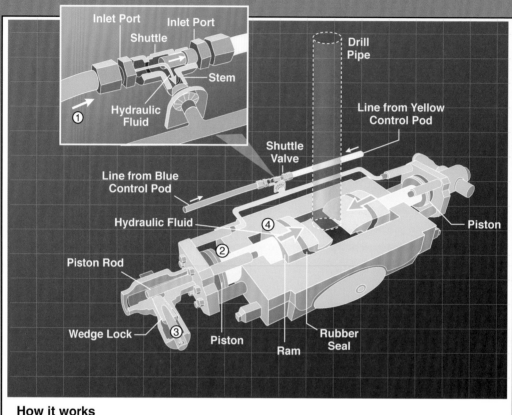

Inlet Port **Inlet Port**
Shuttle
Stem
Hydraulic Fluid
①

Drill Pipe

Line from Yellow Control Pod

Shuttle Valve

Line from Blue Control Pod

Hydraulic Fluid

④

②

Piston Rod

Piston

Wedge Lock
③
Piston
Ram
Rubber Seal

How it works

① Fluid enters the shuttle valve from one of two inlet ports and pushes a metal "shuttle" to one side and flows down the stems of the T-shaped valve.

② The fluid flows behind pistons, which drive the ram to shear the drill pipe.

③ Wedge locks slide in to prevent the pistons from moving back.

④ Rubber seals on the ram close off the well. Oil pushing up from the well adds pressure below and behind the ram, helping to keep the ram closed.

How the Ram Cuts the Drill Pipe

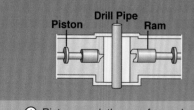

Piston **Drill Pipe** **Ram**

① Pistons push the ram forward

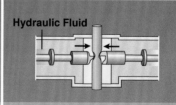

Hydraulic Fluid

② Offset blades on the ram cut

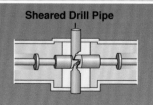

Sheared Drill Pipe

③ The pipe breaks

Source: *New York Times*, "Investigating the Cause of the Deepwater Horizon Blowout," June 21, 2010. www.nytimes.com.

450-ton apparatus (408 metric tons) that contains a number of valves that are supposed to shut when an unexpected gusher emerges from the seabed. For the blowout preventer to work, the well pipe must be sheared off. This operation had to be initiated in the control room of the *Deepwater Horizon*—which at the time was exploding in flames. Rig workers in the control room initiated the switch to shear off the pipe and, with their lives in danger, fled the rig and headed to safety. A mile below the platform, the pipe did not shear all the way off. As a result, the valves in the blowout preventer could not close. Investigators believe something got in the way of the cutting device—probably chunks of cement or other debris. A few feet below, another failsafe feature in the blowout preventer went into action: a ramming device designed to break through the pipe and seal off the flow. The rams failed as well; evidently, the rams hit a pipe joint, which was too thick for them to break through.

What analysts find remarkable about the catastrophe is that the *Deepwater Horizon* lacked a remote switch that would have given the control room operators additional chances to shear off the pipe. After they fled the rig, the operators could have triggered the switch from a lifeboat. U.S. regulations did not require BP to employ the remote switch, but in other countries they are mandatory. Officials from Dutch, French, and Brazilian regulatory agencies all said they require the use of remote switches in the event the control room personnel have to evacuate the rig. "Our concern is both safety and the environment,"[74] says Raphael Moura, head of safety for the National Petroleum Agency of Brazil.

Ironically, the MMS became aware of the deficiencies in blowout preventers a decade before the *Deepwater Horizon* explosion. In 2000 the agency produced a study of 151 well blowouts since 1975 (most were minor, occurring in shallow water) and concluded that the blowout preventers were ill-designed and that, if a blowout occurred in deep water, it could take months to seal the well. "Of particular concern is the ability to stop a blowout once it has begun,"[75] concluded the MMS report. Ten years before the *Deepwater Horizon* catastrophe, the MMS study had correctly predicted what could happen in a worst-case scenario should a blowout occur in deep water and the blowout preventer fail. Sadly, the MMS failed to act on this vital information.

Possible Design Changes

The efforts to redesign the blowout preventer are expected to focus on the ramming device that failed to break through the pipe joint. In the redesigned blowout preventer, the rams would be made bigger and more powerful. That is an essential redesign, experts believe, because while the design of the blowout preventers have not changed over the past 30 years, the pipe used to channel oil out of the seabed has gotten much stronger, thanks to advancements in metallurgy. In other words, the ability of the rams to break through the pipe did not keep up with the ability of the pipe to withstand external forces.

In the meantime, some industry officials have advocated that all wells feature two blowout preventers—one stationed at the

An image from a live video feed on the BP Web site shows the oil plume spewing from the sunken rig shortly before one of several unsuccessful efforts to choke off the gusher. The well was finally capped in September 2010.

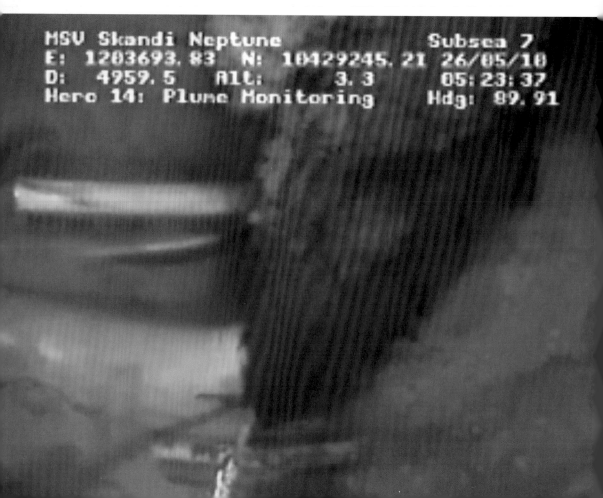

wellhead and the other located just below the platform. Engineers are divided on this strategy. Clearly, to install a second blowout preventer just below sea level, major engineering changes would have to be made to the rig and pipeline to support the new infrastructure. "The cost would be somewhere near prohibitive," says Geoff Kimbrough, vice president for deepwater operations at the Texas-based drilling company New Tech Engineering. "Just the cost to develop the system would be astronomical. Mandating something like that would delay new drilling at least several years. You're talking about years to develop and test and prove something like that."[76]

In response, University of Texas engineering professor Paul Bommer says that even if a second blowout preventer had cost tens of millions of dollars, it may have saved the billions of dollars in damages as well as the environmental catastrophe caused by the *Deepwater Horizon* accident. "Cost is the last thing people should be thinking about now,"[77] he says.

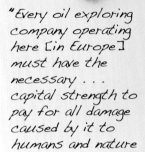

"Every oil exploring company operating here [in Europe] must have the necessary . . . capital strength to pay for all damage caused by it to humans and nature in a worst case scenario."[78]

— Günther Oettinger, European Union energy commissioner in aftermath of 2010 Gulf spill.

Spill Response Plans

Another deficiency uncovered during the catastrophe was the lack of a plan to stop the leak. Indeed, BP tried many techniques for capping the flow before finally finding a method that worked 85 days after the accident. In the meantime, 210 million gallons (795 million L) of crude oil leaked into the Gulf of Mexico. Throughout the catastrophe, the U.S. Coast Guard monitored the operation, but the federal government lacked the expertise, equipment, and resources to cap the leak on its own. Therefore, the government had to rely on BP to cap the leak.

In the future, the federal government is not expected to assume a "first responder" role in the event of another well blowout but, rather, continue to rely on the industry to plug its own leaks. Nevertheless, in the weeks following the *Deepwater Horizon* accident, members of Congress proposed legislation that would require oil companies to develop spill response plans that must be approved by the Coast Guard.

Salvaging the *Deepwater Horizon*

The investigation into what went wrong beneath the *Deepwater Horizon* was aided when crews were able to hoist the rig's blowout preventer to the surface. The painstaking operation was completed four months after the accident that caused 210 million gallons (795 million L) of oil to spill into the gulf. Since the accident, the blowout preventer sat on the seafloor, but crews were able to hoist the 450-ton device (408 metric tons) to the surface using robot submersible crafts as well as a crane aboard a surface vessel.

The oil spilled into the gulf waters because the blowout preventer failed to seal the well. By examining the device, engineers hope to learn why the blowout preventer failed to break through a steel tube that funneled the oil to the surface.

As for the rig itself, the 36,000-ton drilling platform (32,600 metric tons) remains on the seafloor, 5,000 feet (1,524m) below the surface. Investigators are anxious to examine the wreckage to see what may have caused the explosion that killed 11 rig workers. Salvage experts wonder whether a rig that size can ever be raised to the surface. "Five thousand feet is awfully deep," says Malcolm M. MacKinnon III, a retired U.S. Navy admiral and salvage consultant. "To salvage any part of the rig itself I would think would be very close to impossible."

Quoted in Matthew L. Wald, "Raising Remnants of Oil Rig Is Still on the Agenda," *New York Times*, June 8, 2010.

Other Nations Impose New Rules

In the months following the *Deepwater Horizon* spill, the U.S. government was not the only regulator to look closely at the safety features of offshore rigs. In other countries, governments examined the offshore rigs operating off their coasts and saw the potential for similar accidents. Many governments took immediate steps to correct the deficiencies.

The 27 countries of the European Union resolved to ensure that all oil companies drilling offshore along European coastlines possess the financial abilities to pay for the cleanups should new spills occur. "The recent tragedy in the Gulf of Mexico now poses very serious and urgent questions about [offshore] operations," says Günther Oettinger, the European Union energy commissioner. "Every oil exploring company operating here must have the necessary . . . capital strength to pay for all damage caused by it to humans and nature in a worst case scenario."[78]

Meanwhile, individual countries took steps toward enhancing safety at offshore rigs operating in nearby waters. Great Britain doubled all inspections on offshore rigs operating in British waters in the North Sea. Canada imposed new, enhanced safety rules on offshore operators. These rules were imposed mostly with deepwater wells in mind, specifically a well under development by Chevron off the coast of Newfoundland. The Chevron drilling platform sits atop more than 8,500 feet (2,591m) of water; it is the deepest drilling operation in Canadian waters. In China, the

Heavily oiled brown pelicans wait to be cleaned. Nations around the world have committed to strengthening laws in an effort to prevent another catastrophe on the scale of the one that took place in the Gulf of Mexico in 2010.

country's National Offshore Oil Corporation, which is owned by the government of China, says it is upgrading requirements for blowout preventers employed on its rigs. French authorities are taking steps as well: The French oil company Total created task forces to study safety features on its rigs and also draft new contingency plans should spills occur.

From across the globe came not only a great outpouring of sympathy for the people and environment of the Gulf Coast that suffered during the *Deepwater Horizon* spill but also a firm resolve by other political and oil industry leaders not to let similar spills occur off the coasts of their countries. Said the South Korean newspaper *JoongAng*, "The very first victims were the fishermen of Louisiana, but no one on Earth is free from the impact of this disaster."[79]

The Energy Infrastructure

With the energy needs of the United States (and many other countries) still squarely reliant on oil, drilling in the Gulf of Mexico and elsewhere along the American coastline is expected to continue for many decades. Certainly, Americans are making efforts to wean themselves off oil. Electric cars started rolling off the production lines in 2010. Solar, wind, biofuels, and other alternative energy sources are believed to be very much in America's future. So is nuclear power, which is expected to move forward now that the safety questions surrounding the Three Mile Island accident have long since been addressed.

Yet oil will likely remain an important component of the world's energy infrastructure for many years to come. According to the International Energy Agency, the global demand for oil may rise by as much as 70 percent by 2050—and offshore resources will probably be a part of the supply chain. The main issue facing industry leaders, government regulators, and the people who live along the coastlines of their countries, though, is whether that oil can be drawn safely from platforms that float atop thousands of feet of water.

"The very first victims were the fishermen of Louisiana, but no one on Earth is free from the impact of this disaster."[79]

— *JoongAng*, South Korean newspaper, commenting on BP spill.

Facts

- A Norwegian study tested blowout preventers on 11 deepwater wells in the North Sea; the study determined that in six of the wells, the blowout preventers would fail, according to a 2010 report in the journal *Machine Design*.

- A study partially financed by BP suggested that blowout preventers need only be tested every 35 days rather than the industry standard, which is every 14 days, the journal *Machine Design* reported in 2010. The study found that in 90,000 tests of blowout preventers, only 62 had failed.

- Offshore platforms were considered to be among the safest structures along the Gulf Coast because few suffered more than minor damages during Hurricane Katrina, the devastating storm of 2005 that caused billions of dollars in damage to coastal communities.

- Before it was disbanded by the U.S. Interior Department, the Minerals Management Service approved environmental waivers on five offshore drilling projects after the April 20, 2010, *Deepwater Horizon* accident. Four of those approvals were for deepwater wells.

- The first blowout preventers were employed on offshore wells in 1920; engineers say the design of the preventers has basically remained unchanged since then.

- The remote device that could have operated the *Deepwater Horizon* blowout preventer from a lifeboat is about the size of a football and costs about $500,000; its use on offshore rigs is not required under federal law.

Related Organizations and Web Sites

American Petroleum Institute (API)

1220 L St. NW
Washington, DC 20005
phone: (202) 682-8000
Web Site: www.api.org

The API is a trade organization representing oil and gas companies. Visitors to the API Web site can download the document *Deepwater Horizon Questions & Answers—Industry Safety and Responsibility* to learn how safety issues raised by the collapse of the *Deepwater Horizon* platform are being addressed by offshore drillers.

BP

501 Westlake Park Blvd.
Houston, TX 77079
phone: (281) 366-2000
Web site: www.bp.com

Formerly known as British Petroleum, BP is one of the world's largest oil companies. BP owns the rights to the oil field below the *Deepwater Horizon* platform. Students can learn about BP's response to the spill by following a link on the company's Web site to "Gulf of Mexico Response," which features information on how BP capped the well and has organized the cleanup of the Gulf Coast.

Energy Watch Group

Zinnowitzer Strabe 1
10115 Berlin, Germany
phone: +49 (0)30 3988 9664
e-mail: office@energywatchgroup.org
Web site: www.energywatchgroup.org

This is an independent international organization of scientists who monitor energy use and provide energy policy guidance for national leaders. The group's Web site includes the downloadable *Crude Oil: The Supply Outlook*, in which the organization estimates the amount of oil, including offshore resources, available in the future.

Exxon Valdez Oil Spill Trustee Council

441 W. 5th Ave., Suite 500
Anchorage, AK 99501
phone: (800) 478-7745
fax: (907) 276-7178
e-mail: dfg.evos.restoration@alaska.gov
Web site: www.evostc.state.ak.us

The environmental recovery of Prince William Sound is monitored by the council, which administers the fund of $900 million established by ExxonMobil to finance the cleanup. Students can find many resources about the 1989 spill on the organization's Web site by following the link to "Teachers & Students: Oil Spill Facts."

Greenpeace

702 H St. NW, Suite 300
Washington, DC 20001
phone: (800) 326-0959
e-mail: info@wdc.greenpeace.org
Web site: www.greenpeace.org

A vigilant environmental activism group, Greenpeace has monitored the *Deepwater Horizon* spill and cleanup in the Gulf of Mexico. Follow the link on the Greenpeace Web site to "Gulf Oil Spill Impacts Expedition" to read blog entries by activists who have inspected the environmental damage and cleanup activities.

Independent Petroleum Association of America (IPAA)

1201 15th St. NW, Suite 300
Washington, DC 20005
phone: (202) 857-4722
fax: (202) 857-4799
Web site: www.ipaa.org

The IPAA represents American oil and gas companies and lobbies Congress for laws favoring oil and gas exploration. Position papers on the group's Web site explain its opposition to the temporary moratorium on deepwater drilling and its position on other issues that affect offshore exploration.

National Ocean Industries Association (NOIA)

1120 G St. NW, Suite 900
Washington, DC 20005
phone: (202) 347-6900
fax: (202) 347-8650
Web site: www.noia.org

The NOIA is the trade association representing more than 250 companies involved in offshore oil and gas drilling, including oil companies, rig operators, and shipping companies. The link to "Gulf Economic Issues" leads to many reports and other resources detailing the importance of offshore drilling to the economy of the Gulf Coast.

U.S. Bureau of Ocean Energy Management, Regulation and Enforcement (BOEMRE)

1849 C St. NW
Washington, DC 20240
phone: (202) 208-3985
e-mail: BOEMPublicAffairs@BOEMRE.gov
Web site: www.boemre.gov

Formerly the U.S. Minerals Management Service, BOEMRE is responsible for inspecting offshore oil and gas platforms in U.S. waters. Students can download copies of *Ocean Science*, the agency's magazine, which includes numerous articles on ecology and scientific studies in the Gulf of Mexico and other places where offshore drilling occurs.

U.S. Department of Energy (DOE)

1000 Independence Ave. SW
Washington, DC 20585
phone: (202) 586-5000
fax: (202) 586-4403
e-mail: The.Secretary@hq.doe.gov
Web site: www.energy.gov

The DOE monitors the consumption and generation of energy in America. Visitors to the department's Web site can follow the link to the Gulf Coast Oil Spill Resource Center, which provides a timeline of the *Deepwater Horizon* spill as well as updates on DOE's response to the emergency and videos of oil gushing from the open wellhead.

U.S. Department of the Interior (DOI)

1849 C St. NW
Washington, DC 20240
phone: (202) 208-3100
e-mail: feedback@ios.doi.gov
Web site: www.doi.gov

The department oversees the mineral rights owned by the U.S. government for the outer continental shelf (OCS). The link to "Outer Continental Oil and Gas Strategy" leads to information on the availability of U.S. offshore oil, including maps of proposed drilling areas and estimates of oil resources available in the OCS.

U.S. Energy Information Administration (EIA)

1000 Independence Ave. SW
Washington, DC 20585
phone: (202) 586-8800
e-mail: InfoCtr@eia.gov
Web site: www.eia.doe.gov

An agency of the Department of Energy, EIA compiles statistics on energy use and production in America. The Web site's downloadable *Annual Energy Review* provides historical data on use of oil and other energy sources.

U.S. Environmental Protection Agency (EPA)

Ariel Rios Bldg.
1200 Pennsylvania Ave. NW
Washington, DC 20460
phone: (202) 272-0167
Web site: www.epa.gov

The EPA is the federal government's chief watchdog over the environment, responsible for monitoring the Clean Water Act, Clean Air Act, and other laws that regulate energy production and consumption. The "Oil Spill Response" link leads to updates on the extent of the water and air pollution caused by the *Deepwater Horizon* spill.

Woods Hole Oceanographic Institution

266 Woods Hole Rd.
Woods Hole, MA 02543
phone: (508) 548-1400
e-mail: information@whoi.edu
Web site: www.whoi.edu

The nonprofit organization pursues many international projects that study marine biology. Scientists from the institution discovered the 22-mile oil plume (35.4km) submerged in the Gulf of Mexico. The link for "Plume in the Gulf" explains how the plume was discovered and its potential effects on gulf ecology.

Additional Reading

Books

Newt Gingrich and Vince Haley, *Drill Here, Drill Now, Pay Less*. Washington, DC: Regnery, 2008.

Margaret Haerens, ed., *Opposing Viewpoints: Offshore Drilling*. Detroit: Greenhaven, 2010.

Gal Luft and Anne Korin, eds., *Energy Security Challenges for the 21st Century: A Reference Handbook*. Westport, CT: Greenwood, 2009.

Carla Mooney, *Oil Spills and Offshore Drilling*. San Diego: ReferencePoint, 2011.

John Tabak, *Coal and Oil*. New York: Facts On File, 2009.

Robin M. Williams, *The Myth of the Oil Crisis: Overcoming the Challenges of Depletion, Geopolitics, and Global Warming*. Westport, CT: Greenwood, 2008.

Periodicals

Sharon Begley, "What the Spill Will Kill," *Newsweek*, June 14, 2010.

Jason DeParle, "Leading the Way into Deep Water," *New York Times*, August 8, 2010.

Justin Gillis and Leslie Kaufman, "The Corrosive Legacy of Oil Spills," *New York Times*, July 18, 2010.

New York Times, "Obama's Remarks on Offshore Drilling," March 31, 2010.

Evan Thomas and Daniel Stone, "Black Water Rising," *Newsweek*, June 7, 2010.

Brian Walsh, "On the Edge," *Time*, June 14, 2010.

Internet Sources

Center for American Progress, "Where Is Our Oil Coming From?" Interactive map. www.americanprogress.org/issues/2008/05/oil_imports.html/index.html.

The Daily Green, "The Health Effects of Oil Spills." www.thedailygreen.com/environmental-news/latest/oil-spill-health-effects-0510.

gCaptain.com, "History's 10 Most Famous Oil Spills." http://gcaptain.com/maritime/blog/historys-10-most-famous-oil-spills.

Geology.com, "Mineral Rights." http://geology.com/articles/mineral-rights.shtml.

Source Notes

Introduction: Crisis in the Gulf

1. Quoted in Suzanne Goldberg, "Deepwater Horizon Survivor Describes Horrors of Blast and Escape from Rig," *London Guardian*, May 20, 2010. www.guardian.co.uk.

2. Quoted in Goldberg, "Deepwater Horizon Survivor Describes Horrors of Blast and Escape from Rig."

3. Quoted in Philip Sherwell, "BP Disaster: Worst Oil Spill in U.S. History Turns Seas into a Dead Zone," *London Telegraph*, May 29, 2010. www.telegraph.co.uk.

4. Quoted in Friends of the Earth, "Oil Spill Continues to Leak 1,000 Barrels Per Day into Gulf of Mexico," news release, April 27, 2010. www.foe.org.

5. Quoted in *New York Times*, "Obama's Remarks on Offshore Drilling," March 31, 2010. www.nytimes.com.

6. Quoted in CBS News, "Blowout: The Deepwater Horizon Disaster," May 16, 2010. www.cbsnews.com.

7. Quoted in CBS News, "Blowout: The Deepwater Horizon Disaster."

Chapter One: What Are the Origins of the Offshore Oil Controversy?

8. Quoted in Joe R. Nevarez, "Industry Using Several Methods to Combat Underwater Blowouts," *Los Angeles Times*, September 20, 1965, p. B-10.

9. Quoted in *New York Times*, "Experts Gloomy on Oil Leakage," February 25, 1969, p. 27.

10. Quoted in Russell Blinch, "Cuba's Offshore Oil Hopes Rise, U.S. Role Uncertain," Reuters, June 15, 2009. www.reuters.com.

11. Werner Bamberger, "Search for Oil Producing a New 'Sea Monster,'" *New York Times*, January 31, 1965, p. S-18.

12. Quoted in Joe R. Nevarez, "Offshore Crude Now 16 Percent of World Total," *Los Angeles Times*, December 6, 1965, p. B-12.

13. Quoted in William K. Stevens, "Gulf of Mexico in Key Fuel Role," *New York Times*, May 3, 1979, p. D-1.

14. Quoted in Colby Frazier, "Locals Remember Oil Spill Like It Was Yesterday," *Santa Barbara Daily Sound*, January 28, 2009. www.thedailysound.com.

15. Quoted in Jessica Lyons, "Disaster Déjà Vu," *San Jose Metro*, July 28, 2010. www.metroactive.com.

16. Quoted in Jason DeParle, "Leading the Way into Deep Water," *New York Times*, August 8, 2010, p. 12.

17. Quoted in Warren Brown, "Oil Spill Threatens Texas Coast," *Washington Post*, August 8, 1979, p. A-5.

18. Quoted in Brent R. Schlender, "Texas Island's Fishermen, Resort Owners Anxiously Chart Course of Large Oil Spill," *Wall Street Journal*, August 9, 1979, p. 27.

19. E.F. Loveland, "Energy for the Eighties," *Vital Speeches of the Day*, August 15, 1980, p. 653.

Chapter Two: Is America's Energy Security Dependent on Offshore Oil?

20. Quoted in *Washington Post*, "Arabs to Cut Oil Flow to U.S.," October 18, 1973, p. A-7.

21. Quoted in John Cassidy, "Pump Dreams," *New Yorker*, October 11, 2004. www.newyorker.com.

22. Jack Gerard, "New Drilling Ban Shortsighted," *National Journal*, July 12, 2010. http://energy.nationaljournal.com.

23. Phillip E. Cornell, "Energy Security as National Security: Defining Problems Ahead of Solutions," *Journal of Energy Security*, February 2009. www.ensec.org.

24. Quoted in Hugh Collins, "Chavez Threatens to Cut Oil Exports to U.S. If Colombia Attacks," Daily Finance, July 26, 2010. www.dailyfinance.com.

25. Quoted in Beth Braverman, "McCain: U.S. Needs 'Energy Security,'" CNN, June 18, 2008. http://money.cnn.com.

26. Quoted in *New York Times*, "Obama's Remarks on Offshore Drilling."

27. Randall Luthi, "A View from Washington: The Winds of Change," *Offshore*, May 2010, p. 98.

28. Newt Gingrich and Vince Haley, *Drill Here, Drill Now, Pay Less*. Washington, DC: Regnery, 2008, pp. 5–6.

29. Quoted in Sam Stein, "Bill Nelson: Energy Bill with Offshore Drilling 'Dead on Arrival,'" *Huffington Post,* April 30, 2010. www.huffingtonpost.com.

30. Quoted in Margaret Talev and Kevin G. Hall, "Obama: Drilling Is Just Part of the Strategy," *Philadelphia Inquirer*, April 1, 2010, p. A-9.

31. Quoted in Wilderness Society, "Arctic Drilling Plan Gets Green Light; Analysis of Impacts Sorely Lacking," December 8, 2009. http://wilderness.org.

32. *Scholastic News*, "Should We Drill?" April 26, 2010, p. 5.

33. Byron Dorgan and George Voinovich, "National Energy and Security Act Allows U.S. to Make Dramatic Reduction in Oil Dependence," *The Hill*, June 24, 2009, p. 30.

34. Quoted in Jed Babbin, "House Republican Rebellion Continues," *Human Events*, August 5, 2008. www.humanevents.com.

35. Quoted in Lola Sherman, "Gulf Oil Spill Reignites Question of Offshore Drilling in California," *East County Magazine*, May 6, 2010. www.eastcountymagazine.org.

Chapter Three: Can the Environment Recover from Offshore Drilling Accidents?

36. Quoted in Beth Daley, "Damage Lives on from 1969 Cape Oil Spill," *Boston Globe*, May 21, 2010. www.boston.com.

37. Quoted in Justin Gillis and Leslie Kaufman, "The Corrosive Legacy of Oil Spills," *New York Times*, July 18, 2010, p. 1.

38. Quoted in John Merritt, "The Last Frontier Defiled," *London Observer*, April 2, 1989, p. 15.

39. Quoted in Gillis and Kaufman, "The Corrosive Legacy of Oil Spills," p. 16.

40. Quoted in Gillis and Kaufman, "The Corrosive Legacy of Oil Spills," p. 16.

41. Quoted in Bryan Welsh, "On the Edge," *Time*, June 14, 2010, p. 36.

42. Quoted in Rachel Streitfield, "Oil Disaster Deadly for Gulf Wildlife," CNN, June 8, 2010. www.cnn.com.

43. Quoted in Seth Borenstein, "Fears Oil Mess Lurks Underwater," *Philadelphia Inquirer*, August 19, 2010, p. A-8.

44. Quoted in Sharon Begley, "What the Spill Will Kill," *Newsweek*, June 14, 2010, p. 28.

45. Quoted in Gillis and Kaufman, "The Corrosive Legacy of Oil Spills," p. 16.

46. Quoted in Allison Ross, "Crowds Link Hands to Fight Drilling," *Palm Beach Post*, June 27, 2010, p. 1B.

47. Quoted in Jeff Barker, "Hands Across the Sand Stretches Across Beaches to Protest Offshore Drilling, Promote Clean Energy," *Northwest Florida Daily News*, June 27, 2010. www.nwfdailynews.com.

48. Quoted in Maggie Fitzroy, "Taking a Stand with Hands Across the Sand," *Florida Times Union*, June 30, 2010, p. L-1.

49. Quoted in NTDTV, "Greenpeace Stages Oil Drill Protest," July 22, 2010. http://english.ntdtv.com.

50. Quoted in Gillis and Kaufman, "The Corrosive Legacy of Oil Spills," p. 17.

51. Quoted in Gillis and Kaufman, "The Corrosive Legacy of Oil Spills," p. 17.

52. Quoted in Cain Burdeau and Jeffrey Collins, "Oil-Fouled Marshes Starting to Renew on Louisiana Coast," *Philadelphia Inquirer*, August 12, 2010, p. A-2.

53. Quoted in Seth Borenstein, "A 22-Mile Oil Plume Is Deep in Cold Gulf," *Philadelphia Inquirer*, August 20, 2010, p. A-9.

Chapter Four: Do the Economic Benefits of Offshore Drilling Outweigh the Risks?

54. Quoted in Rong-Gong Lin Il, "Gulf Oil Spill: Pro-Drilling Rally Pushes Back at Obama Moratorium," *Los Angeles Times*, July 21, 2010. http://latimesblogs.latimes.com.

55. Quoted in Lin Il, "Gulf Oil Spill: Pro-Drilling Rally Pushes Back at Obama Moratorium."

56. Quoted in MSNBC, "Alaska Residents Cash In on Annual Dividend," September 5, 2008. www.msnbc.msn.com.

57. Quoted in Frank Morris, "Oil, Fishing Industries Entwined in Mississippi River Delta," NPR, June 3, 2010. www.npr.org.

58. Quoted in Josh Harkinson, "Oil Rigs and the Fishermen Who Love Them," *Mother Jones*, June 24, 2010. http://mother jones.com.

59. Quoted in Harkinson, "Oil Rigs and the Fishermen Who Love Them."

60. Quoted in Donna Leinwand, "Gulf Spill Takes Bite Out of Restaurants," *USA Today*, June 23, 2010. www.usatoday.com.

61. Quoted in Noaki Schwartz, "Beaches Clean, but Tourist Perceptions Tainted," *Philadelphia Inquirer*, August 23, 2010, p. A-3.

62. Quoted in Schwartz, "Beaches Clean, but Tourist Perceptions Tainted," p. A-3.

63. Carolyn McCormick, "Perspectives on the Outer Continental Shelf," testimony before the U.S. House Committee on Natural Resources, February 11, 2009. http://resourcescommittee.house.gov.

64. W.F. Grader Jr., "Offshore Drilling: Environmental and Commercial Perspectives," testimony before the U.S. House Committee on Natural Resources, February 11, 2009. http://resourcescommittee.house.gov.

65. Quoted in Sherman, "Gulf Oil Spill Reignites Question of Offshore Drilling in California."

66. American Petroleum Institute, "Second to None: The U.S. Offshore Industry's Safety and Environmental Records," March 10, 2009. www.api.org.

67. Quoted in Rick Jervis, William M. Welch, and Richard Wolf, "Worth the Risk? Debate on Offshore Drilling Heats Up," *USA Today*, July 14, 2008. www.usatoday.com.

Chapter Five: Can Offshore Drilling Be Made Safer?

68. Helen Thorpe, "Oil & Water," *Texas Monthly*, February 1996, p. 88.

69. Quoted in DeParle, "Leading the Way into Deep Water," p. 12.

70. Quoted in Kathrine Schmidt, "In Wake of Disaster, Drilling Is Examined," *Lafourche Parish* (LA) *Daily Comet*, May 30, 2010. www.dailycomet.com.

71. Quoted in DeParle, "Leading the Way into Deep Water," p. 12.

72. Quoted in States News Service, "Salazar Swears-In Michael R. Bromwich to Lead Bureau of Ocean Energy Management, Regulation and Enforcement," June 21, 2010.

73. Quoted in John M. Broder, "Tougher Rules for Drilling Permits," *Philadelphia Inquirer*, August 17, 2010, p. A-7.

74. Quoted in Russell Gold, Ben Casselman, and Guy Chazan, "Leaking Oil Well Lacked Safeguard Device," *Wall Street Journal*, April 28, 2010. http://online.wsj.com.

75. Quoted in DeParle, "Leading the Way into Deep Water," p. 13.

76. Quoted in Peter Fairley, "How to Prevent Deepwater Spills," *MIT Technology Review*, June 10, 2010. www.technologyreview.com.

77. Quoted in Fairley, "How to Prevent Deepwater Spills."

78. Quoted in New Europe, "Oettinger's Call for Offshore Drilling Regulation Draws Lukewarm OPEC Response," July 4, 2010. www.neurope.eu.

79. Quoted in Jane Wardell, "Nations Rethink Offshore Drilling," MSNBC, June 20, 2010. www.msnbc.msn.com.

Index